PRIVATE BANKING

Private banking

A global perspective

Lucy Weldon

GRESHAM
BOOKS

WOODHEAD
PUBLISHING
LIMITED
IN ASSOCIATION WITH
THE CHARTERED
INSTITUTE OF
BANKERS

Published by Gresham Books, an imprint of Woodhead Publishing Limited,
Abington Hall, Abington, Cambridge CB1 6AH, England

First published 1998

British Library Cataloguing in Publication Data
A catalogue record for this book is available from the British Library.

ISBN 1 85573 328 5

Typeset by BookEns Ltd, Royston, Herts.
Printed by TJ International, Cornwall, England.

Contents

Introduction

When writing this book, I had in mind a number of things which have shaped its structure and content. In all my initial research, there appeared to be nothing available on the private banking industry, both domestic and international, that clearly established its evolution and predicted its future. Information is generally piecemeal and disconnected, particularly on the international side. Given the opaqueness that has always surrounded the industry, information until recently has been based largely on supposition and opinion. The recent moves within the industry towards greater transparency were long overdue!

Furthermore, despite concurrent developments in international and domestic private banking, little had been written about the relationship between the two business lines. Given that a number of providers actively pursue both types of market, this is surprising. Moreover, within international private banking, regional perspectives are all too common and often Europe centred. This means that the complex relationships between the different parts of the globe where products, servicing and wealth management styles are disparate are not always understood and nor are the dynamics of the different regions.

Therefore, I have written this book with the aim of addressing these points as far as possible. Importantly, the book has been written:

- to provide an authoritative overview of the industry today;

- to highlight key issues and trends facing the industry;
- and to explore the likely development of the industry over the next decade.

The book should be of interest to private bankers looking for a global perspective.

I should mention also what the book is not going to cover. It is not a text to help technical experts looking for help on the 'ins' and 'outs' of products, law and regulations, investment management and so on. The focus of the book is the market as defined by wealth, clients, providers and the major components of the operating environment.

Putting together the book has required a number of approaches. Domestic private banking was straightforward because it is essentially a transparent line of business where performance and dimensions are becoming routinely reported and where professional research is regularly undertaken on the market. International private banking, on the other hand, proved to be more problematic and needed a number of checks and balances to ensure accurate and relevant information.

The principle of approach has been to get first-hand information from industry experts through interviews. The interview programme was designed to be representative of the industry, so providers were looked at according to type, origin and size as well as geographic and product specialisation. This meant that providers ranged from the largest - both US and Swiss, to the more medium-sized European providers and the specialists. Broad geographic representation has been largely achieved, with interviews conducted all around the world including Brazil, Hong Kong, Zürich, London, Bahrain, Singapore and New York. The interviewees ranged from private bankers in the front line, to functional experts such as investment managers through to chief executives. In addition, these were complemented by interviews with those who provide support for the industry such as management consultants, lawyers, tax experts, staff of research companies, analysts and economists.

There are two distinctive parts to the book; the first covering international private banking and the second covering domestic private banking. Although different, the two are closely linked. The book has been structured in the following way:

- It starts by looking at wealth and the key dynamics of wealth that are relevant to both international and domestic private banking.
- The international side of the industry is then reviewed and the

geographical regions of Asia-Pacific, Europe, the Americas and the Middle East profiled.

- A worldwide perspective of domestic private banking is provided with market studies of two of the leading domestic markets, the USA and the UK.
- The last chapter looks at the binding themes and future challenges for the industry as a whole.

However, one of the general issues that relate to both domestic and international private banking is one of definition. Definition matters because it enables the market to recognise the service offering as appropriate or otherwise, the industry to establish a common set of characteristics against which to compete and compare, and the individual providers to understand what the term precisely means for them and their part of the market. It is increasingly clear that the term private banking now encompasses a much wider field and has become more a description of the market and level of service provided. The seamless requirement throughout the market is for high-quality service, dedicated attention and a range of wealth management services. It is important to cut the ties with the past definition with its associations with certain providers and cultures, and to look forward.

Acknowledgements

I am indebted to a number of people who have given me help in writing this book:

- Madeleine Donovan, Joanne Ashcroft, Anna Ellison, David Pitman and Julio Harari.
- A number of management consultants and research and advisory companies:

  Gemini Consulting (London)
  Price Waterhouse (London)
  Bain and Co (London)
  Bain and Co (Singapore)
  Deloitte Touche Tohmatsu International (London)
  Towers Perrin (New York)
  PSI (Florida)
  Advisory Board (Washington DC)
  Prospektus (London)

- The interviewees who not only met me once, but also answered follow-up questions, made introductions for me and reviewed the texts.
- Alan Richards and Lou-lou Richards.

- My parents, Brian and Angela Weldon, for baby *amah* services rendered.

I would also like to add in a few of my key observations arising from the interviews: the Swiss providers are a controversial subject; the industry had been languishing until competition recently pulled it up by its boot straps; there is a lot of theatre in private banking that needs de-bunking; wealth and wealthy people can be alluring subjects; the future opportunity is already being grasped firmly by providers of all sizes; and focus is of key importance.

Lucy Weldon

CHAPTER ONE

Wealth – a worldwide perspective

Introduction

Before looking at the industry at a domestic and international level and at the individual markets, it is important to identify some of the underlying factors and the dynamics of wealth, particularly in the higher echelons of wealth, usually described as high net worth wealth. The growth and the changes that are taking place in the 1990s are creating one of the most important markets in financial services worldwide, namely private banking. From both an international and a domestic perspective, the message is consistent – high net worth wealth is growing rapidly worldwide, and so is private banking as an industry.

The nature and size of wealth differs from one market to another, and from one region to another, reflecting the various economic and demographic factors and different government practices and policies around the world. However, across all the markets, the key shift has been from old wealth to newly created wealth, involving a vastly increased number of individuals and families.

For private bankers, whether working in a domestic or international line of business, these changing dynamics have created a number of new opportunities for providing wealth-management services. The opportunities today and in the future centre on a rapidly growing marketplace, the passing on of wealth from one generation to another and an increasingly segmented market where the new wealth holders are typically younger, more sophisticated and altogether more financially knowledgeable than the older generation.

What has not changed is the overall need for the services of the private banker, whose role is to assist in the optimal management of wealth, finding the appropriate tax and legal conduits to achieve this end. However, the private banking industry must respond to new requirements of the wealthy, reflecting the change in generation, the expansion of the market and the more diverse sources of wealth, which is either entirely personal or, as increasingly is the case, tied up in privately owned businesses.

The key difference between international and domestic wealth management relates to where the wealth holder is domiciled and resident for tax purposes. Domestic private banking generally provides services to resident, domiciled individuals, whereas international private banking provides services to non-domicile, non-resident individuals, confirming the fact that, despite the forces of globalisation, national fiscal policies remain a primary consideration for the management of wealth.

Key dynamics of private wealth creation worldwide

Some of the key dynamics of private wealth creation are linked to economic performance, particularly economic growth rates, the stock market and property market performance and liberalising of markets. Demographic factors are also relevant, such as changes in a market's socio-economic profile, age and distribution of population. Furthermore, government policies, especially those on taxation, pension and healthcare planning, and on incentives for new business creation, all have a direct bearing on growth of private wealth and also on whether this wealth is managed domestically or internationally.

The summary of regional characteristics (Table 1.1) aims to capture the essence and the contrasting features of the various regions. The fuller story is found in the market profiles given later in this book. However, for high net wealth, the key dynamics today can be summarised as:

- Rapid growth of high net worth individual wealth during the decade 1986–96.
- Rebalance of wealth distribution towards Asia.

Table 1.1 Summary of key regional characteristics of private wealth

Asia:	Dominance of overseas Chinese as wealth creators and holders Rapid economic growth of certain emerging markets High savings rates High levels of wealth held internationally
Europe:	Dominance of old wealth and inheritance Ageing population in some industrialised countries Developing small business culture Wealth held both domestically and internationally
Latin America:	Highly concentrated wealth Liberalisation of markets fuelling wealth creation Relatively low savings rates Rebalancing of wealth held internationally and domestically
Middle East:	Highly concentrated wealth Importance of natural resources and import and export business High levels of wealth held internationally
North America:	Impact of new wealth through business start-ups Ageing population Dominance of the 'baby boomers' Wealth predominantly held and invested domestically

- The coming-of-age of the business entrepreneur.
- Diversity of economic organisations and business sectors involved in wealth creation.
- The ageing population and the skewing of wealth.
- Growing equity culture and international profile of wealth.

Growth of high net worth individual wealth

In 1996, it was estimated that assets held by high net worth individuals, defined as individuals with net worth of at least $1 million, totalled $16.6 trillion, more than double the 1986 estimate of $7.2 trillion. Apart from Africa, all regions have shown phenomenal growth in high net worth assets over the decade 1986–96. Regionally, Asia, North America and Europe account for the lion's share of high net worth individual wealth. The largest growth over the decade has been in Asia where markets such as South Korea, Hong Kong, Singapore and Taiwan are growing particularly fast.

Table 1.2 High net worth (HNW) assets* by source region 1986–96

Region where wealth sourced	HNW assets 1986 ($ trillion)	HNW assets 1996 ($ trillion)	Change 1986–96 (%)	Region's share of total (%)
Africa	0.3	0.4	+ 33	2
Middle East	0.6	1.1	+ 83	7
Latin America	1.2	2.2	+ 83	13
Asia	0.8	3.5	+337	21
North America	2.3	4.4	+ 91	27
Europe	2.0	5.0	+150	30
Total	7.2	16.6	+130	

* High net worth individuals are defined as those having at least $1 million of net worth.

Source: Gemini Lorenz Curve Analysis; *World Wealth Report 1997*, Gemini Consulting and Merrill Lynch.

The apparent relatively slower growth of wealth sourced from North America can be explained by the devaluation of the US dollar that took place from 1985, rather than by any fundamental slow-down in growth. Nevertheless, there has been a shift in dominance, in terms of largest wealth pool, from West to East. The 1980s saw the dominance of North America as a major source of private wealth; in the 1990s, Europe has become the dominant wealth pool. The pool of high net worth wealth is expected to approach $25 trillion by 2000, with Europe, Asia and North America remaining the dominant wealth pools.

Economic performance and the dominance of Asian emerging markets

Predictions of Asia accounting for 50% of world GNP by 2020[1] reinforce assertion that the leading edge of world economic performance is shifting regionally and explain why the attention of private bankers is turning increasingly towards Asia. Asian emerging market economic performance compared with that of rich industrial countries has been particularly remarkable over a 25-year period.

It is predicted that by 2000, Asia will overtake North America, becoming the second-largest source of high net worth wealth behind Europe with an estimated $6.1 trillion of high net worth assets.

Table 1.3 Growth of GDP in Asian emerging markets

Emerging market	GDP per head ($) 1995	GDP growth: annual average (%) 1970–79	1980–89	1990–96
Hong Kong	23900	9.2	7.5	5.0
Singapore	22600	9.4	7.2	8.3
Taiwan	13200	10.2	8.1	6.3
South Korea	11900	9.3	8.0	7.7
Malaysia	10400	8.0	5.7	8.8
Thailand	8000	7.3	7.2	8.6
Indonesia	3800	7.8	5.7	7.2
China	3100	7.5	9.3	10.1
Philippines	2800	6.1	1.8	2.8
Rich industrial countries	19400	3.4	2.6	2.0

* At purchasing power parity.

Sources: IMF, ING Barings, national statistics.

The coming-of-age of the business entrepreneur

It could be said that the business entrepreneur has come of age in the late 20th century and is an increasingly visible and major economic driver across all regions.[2] However, the entrepreneur *per se* is nothing new and has always been prevalent in society. The major difference today, though, is that the energies of the entrepreneur are responding to the spreading of wealth across the globe and the new economic opportunities presented by the demise of communism in favour of capitalism and open market policies. Research on affluent individuals worldwide also confirms the impact of the business entrepreneurs, identifying business wealth as by far the largest contributor to global wealth today.[3] However, theories abound on what helps to produce business entrepreneurs - is it a particular cultural trait, is it the political policies and economic incentives designed to facilitate business creation and growth, is it social structure, or is it a combination of all these factors?

From an examination of three contrasting regions, it is clear that there is no single blueprint but perhaps a short list of facilitating factors. Take the Chinese entrepreneur. Much has been made of 'Asian values' and how they are, debatably, contributing to Asia's economic success.[4] In Chinese societies and not solely in Asia, virtually all private sector businesses are family owned and managed. If incorporated, the business typically will look like a modern corporation but in most cases will be family managed and financed. Chinese family businesses, which operate within a web of family relationships and contacts, have been the bedrock of Asian business. Yet, despite the significant amounts of wealth controlled by ethnic Chinese, no Chinese family firm appears in the list of the world's 100 biggest companies by market capitalisation, even though at least 12 families are estimated to be worth $5 billion or more.[5]

On the other hand, in Europe, where social structure does not play such a significant part in family businesses, it has been argued that it is hard for entrepreneurs - a growing force in the private banking marketplace - to raise capital and harder for small firms to survive, with regulation, taxation and social obligations getting in the way of success. Although there appears to be no shortage of venture capital, most of it is going into management buy-outs of family-owned firms and only about 6% has been invested in start-ups. However, in the past two years, a number of stock markets for small firms have been established in the UK, France, Belgium, the Netherlands, Ireland and Germany, as well as a pan-European stock market - EASDAQ (European Association of Securities Dealers Automated Quotation System). All pale in comparison with the equivalent in the USA (NASDAQ), which has 5036 American companies listed as well as 394 foreign ones. The Alternative Investment Market (AIM) in London is by far the largest small-company stock market, with 265 companies listed and a market capitalisation of $9.3 billion. Others such as the Nouveau Marché in Paris, EASDAQ in Brussels and Neuer Markt in Frankfurt have only a handful of companies listed between them - but it is still early days.

In contrast, the number of new business start-ups in the USA grows by an estimated 20% a year. Importantly, no European firm has the same immediate access to a market of 270 million customers, who speak the same language, use the same currency and have the same business regulations and entrepreneurial culture. The new-business phenomenon in the USA has been characterised principally by the technology sector, particularly the personal computer industry. More than 70% of these technology firms that were started up between 1981 and 1990 were backed by venture capitalists, helping the industry to grow during that period to $100 billion in value.[6]

The part that infrastructure plays in the USA in harnessing the entrepreneurial spirit and helping individuals to start up businesses cannot be overemphasised, and nor should the importance of social structure such as the family, which acts as an economic cohesive force particularly in Chinese family businesses. Arguably, a key factor is a facilitative environment, which can compensate for the lack of certain distinctive cultural characteristics peculiar to Asian markets and best exemplified in Chinese businesses. However, it is clear that whether in the USA or Europe or among overseas Chinese, entrepreneurs are not just born and there is little homogeneity worldwide as to what facilitates the development of entrepreneurs and the setting up of businesses. Undoubtedly, financing, market liberalisation and the attitude towards risk of both entrepreneur and financier all matter.

Diversity of economic organisation and business structure in wealth creation

Businesses that drive wealth creation are diverse in their structure and origins, focus, economic impact and funding. The ways in which businesses create wealth are influenced by a number of factors, such as culture and social structure, together with government and regulatory incentives. The vast majority of businesses, both historically and now, are family ones and form the bulk of small and medium-sized businesses.[7] However, conglomerates too in certain economies can be the dominant force behind growth and signal a departure from small and medium-sized family owned organisations.

- Japan was one of the first countries in East Asia to move beyond family businesses to the modern corporate form of organisation and governance. The giant industrial conglomerates, which have been the engines of economic growth in Japan (such as Mitsubishi and Sumitomo), operate in one of the business networks called *keiretsu*. These are networks of nominally separate organisations, with a bank or financial institution at their centre, which share capital, technology and personnel in ways not open to firms outside the network. Furthermore, cross-shareholding is commonly practised. The *keiretsu* relationship imposes reciprocal moral obligations in dealing with one another whether in advantageous or less advantageous circumstances and these have been a key element in helping Japan build significant positions in global industries.
- In Korea, *chaebol* is a business network based often on kinship and not centred on a financial institution like the *keiretsu*. The Korean *chaebol* is a diverse conglomerate with holdings in a wide range of sectors from heavy manufacturing and electronics to textiles, insurance and retail. Some of the largest ones

are Samsung, Hyundai and Lucky-Goldstar. Founding members of the *chaebol* are still in the driving seat and still control great concentrations of wealth.

- Italy has a significant family-owned business sector composed of small firms, typically innovative, export-oriented and in many cases high tech, known as the *Terza Italia*. This category has been compared to that of the Chinese family businesses, in that the family structure serves as a source of support for the business.
- In Brazil, the business profile is being reshaped largely through privatisation, take-overs and joint ventures. Family firms, including those founded by European immigrants, have developed in an economic environment characterised by high inflation, protection against import competition and foreign exchange controls. This has forced firms to expand sideways rather than internationally and many have emerged as diversified conglomerates. Today, some of the top family-owned Brazilian companies continue to be highly diversified and are involved in sectors such as financial services, media, construction, cement, mining, paper and pulp, mining and petrochemicals.[8]
- In the Middle East, those individuals and families from the higher social strata including the royal family are the controlling force in economic organisations. It is oil and other natural resources that have been the main economic focus. Such is the dominance of natural resources that the vast majority of world oil export revenues are attributed to the Middle East. Middle Eastern countries occupy the top four positions for oil export revenue, Saudi Arabia being by far the largest exporter with 1995 exports totalling $40.5 billion, followed by Iran, Kuwait and the United Arab Emirates. Similarly, Qatar has the third-biggest proven gas reserves after Russia and Iran. The oil and gas wealth in turn has led to new business opportunities such as supermarkets and car dealerships as local standards of living rise.[9]

Ageing population and skewing of wealth distribution

The developed world is rapidly ageing. Particularly fast ageing rates are found in Japan, the USA and Europe who all show similar rates of increase in the population in the 40–65 years age range. Significantly, in these markets, it is in this age band where most of the savings are.[10]

- In Japan, the fastest-growing segment of the population after 1997 will be that of people over 65 years, and the same is true of Germany.
- In the USA, the 'baby boomers' were the main borrowers of the 1980s, when savings actually fell. However, it is predicted that there will be a steady rise in the high-saving segment over most of the next 20 years. It has been estimated that by 2030, the 'elderly dependency ratio' (people aged over 65 as a fraction of those between 20 and 64 years) will have risen to 36%, from 21% in 1990. Between now and 2020, the number of people over the age of 85 years will double to 7 million.
- Further evidence of the ageing profile and the importance of the elderly as significant wealth holders is seen in the UK where the elderly affluent account for approximately one-third of the high net worth population.

With life expectancy rates extending, there is additional pressure by governments for pensions and health care to be funded privately. This will add a different perspective to the sizeable inheritance and savings in the hands of the elderly, and present new opportunities to providers of private banking services.

Equity culture and international profile of wealth[11]

There has been a decisive shift towards international equity investment (see Fig. 1.1). A number of factors are behind the growing appetite for equities and international diversification, and they centre largely on questions of risk and return and on growing opportunities.

- Barriers to international investment have been steadily falling, including those relating to costs, and information and access to newer markets.
- In the context of lower inflation and interest rates and the growing sophistication of investors, equity investment has become increasingly important in the pursuit of capital growth.
- Benefits of international diversification and attractive returns are becoming obvious. Compared with average annual returns of the US and other developed markets in 1992–96 of between 9% and 15%, certain emerging markets such as Poland, China, Brazil, Hungary and Malaysia are showing high levels of return, with average returns calculated between 20% and 77%.

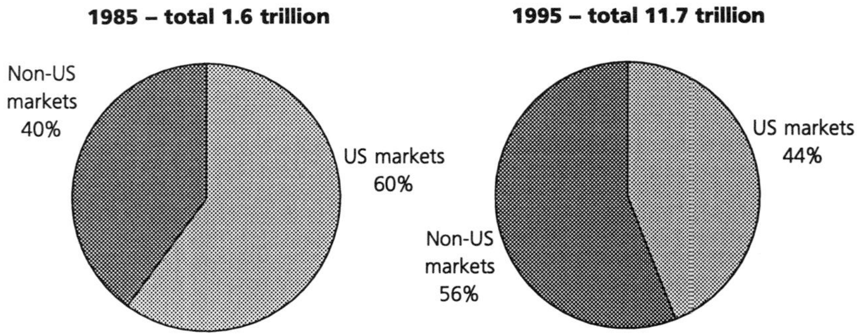

Figure 1.1 Worldwide equity shares traded.
Source: Merrill Lynch.

Key trends and opportunities for private banking

Private bankers are presented with a number of diverse opportunities as a result of changes in market segments. The changes are linked to the passing on of wealth between generations, the important role that the heirs play in private banking and the crossroads that this can present for current private banking clients, and the new market composed of self-made wealthy and of high-salaried individuals and entrepreneurs. The following represent a range of opportunities that are evident across markets, both international and domestic:

- Wealth held by cross-border ethnic groups.
- Inheritors.
- Generational shift in family businesses.
- Wealth in the hands of women.
- High-income earners.

Wealth held by cross-border ethnic groups

There are a number of ethnic groups who transcend traditional geopolitical borders and who represent opportunities for international private banking in particular. Importantly, some of them are significant wealth creators and wealth holders. With their international profile, they actively contribute to the flow of cross-border wealth worldwide. Key characteristics are their extended and scattered families and their international business interests.[12]

- **Non-resident Indians (NRIs):** A survey in 1996 assessed their combined gross assets of $300 billion and net assets of $40–60 billion. Although they are international in their outlook, the liberalisation programme taking place in India is refocusing their attention on financial opportunities there and encouraging them to shift their business and investment interests back towards India. Non-resident Indians, some 15–20 million individuals, populate the professional classes worldwide and their business interests are diverse across Asia, the Middle East, the USA, the UK and East Africa.
- **Overseas Chinese:** there are 57 million Chinese people living outside mainland China; of these, 6 million live outside Asia, in North America, Australia and parts of Europe, with estimated wealth exceeding $2 trillion. Wealth follows the family and relatives and investment opportunities.
- **Muslims:** Islam is the world's second largest religion after Christianity, estimated at 1 billion followers. Markets are geographically spread out beyond the Middle East to include Asia and also to the USA where there are an estimated 5–7 million Muslims. Two key movements in financial services to address this market opportunity have been the rise of Islamic banking and Malaysia's ambitions of establishing Labuan as the leading Islamic offshore centre. Islamic banking is already an established niche banking sector with an estimated worldwide pool of funds of $120 billion.

Inheritors[13]

The profile of world demographics and the ageing profile of certain markets signal that a new generation of inheritors is emerging. The death of parents born during the First World War is now taking place. Inheritances in some cases make heirs wealthy for the first time, and in others compound existing wealth to making them extremely wealthy, particularly where they are already part of super-wealthy families.

Among the more mature economies, it is the USA and UK where there are clear signs of the impact of the scale of inheritance and where these new heirs are identified as a market segment in their own right.

- Reflecting the predominance of old wealth in Europe, this region has a proportionately higher level of inheritances than other regions.

- Research in the USA has identified that 20% of high net worth wealth in USA is the result of inheritance.
- In the UK, inheritors account for approximately 25% of high net worth individuals. A significant proportion of UK inheritance is in the form of property. Typically, this inherited property will be sold, as the heir is often a property owner already. Coupled with a huge rise in property values since the post-war period, the encashment value will propel many UK inheritors towards the rank and file of private banking services for the first time.

Generational shift in family businesses

Many family businesses follow the maxim "shirt sleeves to shirt sleeves in three generations". The business follows a typical pattern of starting with the founding father; after death of the founding father, the children, sometimes only sons, take over; after the death of the children, the business is distributed amongst grandchildren, when the business often disintegrates because of the large number of owners. It is the very nature of a family structure that can be a major constraint on the future success of a business, sometimes preventing them from evolving into durable, large-scale institutions through a desire to keep the business within the management of the family. Furthermore, succession can highlight family squabbles as well as incompetent heirs. Succession and the consequential problems are common throughout a number of markets but the way in which these issues are addressed varies.[14]

- In the USA, 80% of all businesses are family owned and only one-third survive into a second generation, typically being sold and/or moving swiftly into professional corporate management.
- The scale of succession as an issue is seen in Germany where the German Mittelstand businesses too are facing succession problems. Approximately 145 000 businesses are currently managed by owners aged over 65 years, which means that by the year 2000, over a quarter of a million of small to medium-sized businesses in Germany will have to confront the issue of succession. This will be a major transition.
- In Latin America, the succession crossroads faced by family businesses today is in the context of import liberalisation,

lower inflation and the formation of regional trading blocs such as Mercosur, linking Brazil, Argentina, Paraguay and Uruguay. Increasingly, many of the family business empires are beginning to outgrow the ability of their founder to manage them in a more dynamic marketplace as they become more complicated to run.

- In Korea, the heads of *chaebol* groups too are beginning to recognise the importance of bringing in educated corporate managers and are recruiting internationally educated managers, typically with MBAs.

Either way, successful businesses have to face up to the need to have professionally qualified managers, whether family members or from within the corporate ranks, to ensure continuing success. For private bankers, succession in family businesses provides a range of opportunities from tax and estate planning to some new financial planning concepts such as key man insurance through to corporate finance if the family sells out. On the other hand, where relationships with older members of the family have been in place for some time, it is now increasingly the case that the new chains of command are asserting themselves and presenting the private banker with uncertainty over the continuity of the existing relationship, and the competition with an opportunity.

Wealth in the hands of women

The impact of women as key wealth holders in the private banking market is evident in a number of ways and in a number of markets.[15]

- In Asia, there is an emerging generation of women who are professionals, politicians, company presidents, corporate managers and business owners. In particular, statistics indicate that women entrepreneurs across Asia are fast becoming an economic driving force and creators of private wealth. Women are starting and managing small and medium-sized firms in increasing numbers. In Singapore, about 20% of business owners are women. Women have accounted for 25% of all business start-ups in China since 1978. In Japan, women create five out of six new businesses. With rising levels of education and shortage of skilled labour in Asia, the continued importance of women as wealth creators is not expected to diminish.

- In the Middle East, already evident in markets such as Saudi Arabia and the Gulf, is the fact that wealth is increasingly in the hands of women, either through inheritance and/or as the result of business initiatives.

- In the UK, rising education levels and changes in attitude towards marriage and children have propelled women up the earnings tables and women now populate the management levels more densely. As a consequence, what could become of one of the fastest-growing emerging private banking segments in the UK is that of double-income households where women are dominant wealth contributors. Additionally, and not exclusively to the UK, there is the preponderance of wealthy elderly widows made wealthy in their own right by the death of their husband.

High-income earners, professionals and entrepreneurs

Notably, in the more advanced markets a new segment has emerged consisting of high-income earners, many of whom are professionals and high earners in the financial markets, and the self-employed, often described as entrepreneurs. Typically on the domestic private banking side, these are now a distinct group of wealthy individuals, and services are targeted at not just the individuals themselves but also the professional practices, given the close correlation with personal and business wealth.

- In the UK, high-income earners represent one of the smaller wealth segments,[16] estimated at approximately 115 000 individuals in 1995.

- In the USA, there is a noticeable trend in lowering the investment thresholds for private banking services and in developing specially designed services and private banking units for the emerging affluent. The super-regional banks are actively targeting professionals as part of their emerging affluent programmes, focusing on lead products such as credit and simpler investment products and services.

Notes

1 'What drives Deutsche Bank in Asia', *Financial Times*, 13 November 1996.

2 In the 1930s, it was argued that the individual entrepreneur was the key

element in the introduction of the improvements in business methods, organisation and technology which themselves underlie economic growth. J.A. Schumpeter, *The Theory of Economic Development*, Oxford University Press, 1934.

3 Research undertaken by Prince Associates in the USA in 1995 revealed the source of wealth amongst the globally affluent as private business (84.8%), sale of private business (5.8%), inherited wealth (6.4%), employment (1.5%) and other (1.5%).

4 'A conversation with Lee Kuan Yew', *Foreign Affairs*, March/April 1994.

5 *Business in Asia Survey*, 9 March 1996.

6 'Going for the golden egg', *The Economist*, 28 September 1996, p. 124; 'Adventures with capital', *The Economist*, 25 January 1997, p. 15; 'Europe's growth industry', *The Economist*, 15 March 1997, p. 86.

7 Francis Fukoyama, *Trust - The Social Virtues and the Creation of Prosperity*, 1995.

8 'The buying and selling of Brazil Inc.', *The Economist*, 9 November 1997, p. 115; 'The Billionaires - The Americas', *Forbes*, 17 July 1995.

9 'Gushers of money, for a lucky few', *The Economist*, 21 December 1996, p. 78; 'One goes up, the other down', *The Economist*, 8 March 1997, p. 52.

10 'America's amazing strength', *The Economist - The World in 1997*, p. 65; 'The charm of old money', *The Economist*, 15 March 1997, p. 67; *Prospektus (UK)*.

11 'Stay-at-home shareholders', *The Economist*, 17 February 1996, p. 91; 'Low returns, happy returns', *The Economist*, 15 March 1997, p. 88; *Forbes*, 10 February 1997.

12 'Salomon Brothers - primed for success', *Malaysian Business*, 16 February, 1997, p. 35; 'Prophet Sharing', *Wall Street Journal Europe*, 16 February 1996, p. 1, Geoff Hiscock, *Asia's Wealth Club*, p. 137.

13 *Winning Strategies for Private Banking in Asia*, Bain & Company, 2 December 1996; interview with PSI (USA); *Prospektus (UK)*.

14 'Where next for the Mittelstand?', *Private Banker International*, March 1996, p. 9; 'The buying and selling Brazil Inc.', *The Economist*, 9 November 1996, p. 118.

15 John Naisbitt, *Megatrends Asia*, Chapter 7, 'From male dominance - emergence of women'.

16 Inland Revenue statistics, 1994/95, *Prospektus UK*.

CHAPTER TWO

International private banking – a worldwide perspective

Introduction

How times have changed. In the past, it was enough for an international private banking provider to be Swiss. Now, this is no longer sufficient. Today, providers are competing on a more level playing field. Despite the more evenness of hand, competitors differ in capability, type, market focus and size. Such is the diversity that the industry today bears little resemblance to the industry of the past, reflecting the transition taking place within the international private banking marketplace.

Much the same could be said of the clients, in that the industry, which was born out of a 'survivor' mentality, is now addressing a market with a forthright service and performance mentality. The traditional purpose of international private banking was to protect and hold the assets of wealthy individuals who feared the worst and many were indeed living in uncertain times. The international private bank provided an insurance policy in the form of a safe haven. The safe haven is still an important part of the proposition. However, the emphasis has changed and international private banking is now infinitely more complex with greatly extended breadth and depth of products and services and performance requirements.

Growth of the market is continuing to attract new providers and such is the fragmented nature of the industry that there is still a steady inflow. The only truly dominant providers are the three largest Swiss commercial banks, Swiss Bank Corporation (SBC), Union Bank of Switzerland (UBS) and Crédit Suisse. Their longevity in the market and, until more recently, the lack of strong competition, have secured them a clear lead as by far the largest providers of private banking services. However, size does not always correlate to profitability nor is it a sure fast route to success in all markets. Smaller providers too can be successful, because the heart of private banking is still the relationship between provider and client.

External forces in support of international private banking

The recent increased level of competitor activity indicates a high level of confidence in the existing market. In the past, international private banking has thrived on political instability, fluctuating national economic performance and restrictive regulatory and legislative practices. These factors often determined whether a wealthy individual kept his or her assets within national boundaries or moved them outside. Whether or not the crossing of borders was done legally is a mute point. Today, though, there is a number of growing forces that are changing the dynamics and emphasis of international private banking. These forces relate to the mobility of wealth, international investment and transparency of wealth.

Mobility of wealth[1]

In the past, one of the overriding reasons for taking money offshore was lack of stability and fear of appropriation if it was kept onshore. But wealth is continuing to move offshore, in increasing volumes. Statistics reveal that in 1996 some $5.5 trillion of assets were invested offshore, compared with an estimated $2.3 trillion in 1989. There is now, it is believed, a higher level of legitimate flow as a result of a worldwide relaxation in legislative and regulatory practices, particularly from the mid 1980s onwards. In 1985, 38 countries imposed restrictive exchange controls; by 1995, only 11 did so. However, in a number of countries capital restrictions do still exist, or at least formal notification of capital movements over a certain level is required.

Wealth flows in a number of different ways and there is a strong and fluid relationship between offshore and onshore wealth. Repatriation of wealth is largely a function of changed circumstances and economic, social and political stability and has been a characteristic of the 1990s, particularly in regions where instability has been common for some time. Latin America is a good example of where the regional outlook has vastly improved and private wealth is being re-invested domestically (see Chapter 5). In both Asia and Latin America, local investment opportunities are often realised through offshore vehicles.

Instability and the threat of instability are still factors influencing decisions on whether to place or maintain monies offshore. However, in contrast with fifty years ago, a period of time that is still relevant to the older generation of international private banking clients, the world today is comparatively at peace. Since the Second World War, with the stabilising effect of NATO, the Warsaw Pact and the significant development of nuclear weapons, the most powerful nations have been prevented from entering into wars of an even remotely similar scale. Other changes that have contributed to greater stability have been the end of communism in East Europe and the end of military regimes across Latin America. However, even though political and economic stability is much more in evidence, long periods of past instability are still remembered. This continues to add to the mobility of wealth today, particularly in the case of the older generation of private banking clients where the heart can still rule the head with regards to wealth held offshore and the safe haven concept is still held strongly.

Increased levels of international investment[2]

International investment is contributing to the mobility of wealth. The growing level of international investment is a function of both supply and demand and not least is a response to the merits of global diversification that have been promulgated for some time. On the supply side, developments in technology and communications have enabled wealth to be much more mobile, creating the 'global' financial market. Better information on markets and opportunities can be provided as well as the development and distribution of innovative products such as derivatives. Investment products themselves have expanded significantly to include a whole host of alternatives from emerging market funds, new types of funds and new stock markets, all of which could have a place in the product portfolio of an international private banking provider.

The general trend to more international investment is under way in line with growth and development of the international capital markets. The change is already noted in the USA, one of the largest wealth pools in the world.

- Where once US investors were parochial in their investment outlook, with more than 90% of their assets invested at home in the early 1990s, their purchases of foreign securities increased in value by 46% between 1994 and 1995.
- Since 1990 there has been a 21% annual compound growth rate in US investor holdings of foreign equities.
- US investment in international stock funds has also risen significantly, accounting for 10% of all money invested by US investors in stock funds in the first half of 1996, up from 6% in 1995.

Notwithstanding the above, domestic investment can still be attractive for international private banking clients if strong returns are possible, and sometimes this is coupled with a strong client preference to have some wealth close to home.

Another factor contributing to the trend of international investment is economic performance and the impact that currencies, inflation and interest rates can have on an individual's private wealth. Underpinning the growing trend towards international equities is the lowering of interest and inflation rates (see Fig. 2.1 and 2.2). Used to higher returns not so long ago, international private banking clients are now being forced to consider different products in pursuit of similar rates of return. This typically means higher-risk and equity-based products where real returns (as opposed to nominal returns) have become more evident, rather than deposits.

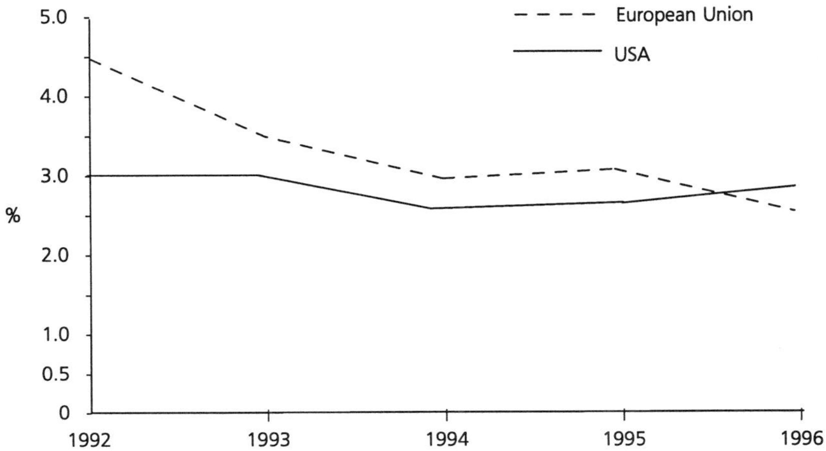

Figure 2.1 Inflation rates 1992–96.
Source: OECD

Figure 2.2 Industrial countries' national interest rates 1992–96 – Treasury Bill rates.
Source: IMF

Greater transparency of wealth[3]

Given the large fiscal deficits that exist in many countries, there has been a decisive shift from governments to become more efficient in collecting taxes whether in Latin America, to address huge fiscal deficits, or in Europe, in anticipation of European Monetary Union. Governments worldwide have been taking measures and providing incentives to encourage individuals to pay their taxes, including the following:

- Simplifying and reducing the personal tax burden.
- Revenue services upgrading their information technology to build up automated histories of tax payers.
- Extension of information links through information exchange provisions in tax treaties to aid identification of tax evaders.
- Introducing tax amnesties.
- Reduction in penal rates of personal taxes. During the period 1975-85, 48 countries imposed top marginal tax rates of 60% or more; by 1994, only 10 imposed such high rates.
- In the case of some authorities, taking matters into their own hands and seizing bank records on grounds of suspicion of tax evasion, as has happened recently in Germany.

However, capital gains, inheritance tax and estate duties are of increasing concern to the internationally wealthy. Whilst the burden of personal income tax may be shifting slightly, and this must be welcome news for individuals declaring income and capital gains domestically, many internationally wealthy clients are more concerned avoiding wealth taxes such as inheritance and gift taxes and estate duties. Wealth taxes account for 2% of total tax receipts in OECD (Organisation for Economic Co-operation and Development) economies.

Additionally, origins of wealth can be an important factor in providing the motivation to declare wealth, particularly if a business has been acquired or there has been an inheritance. The heir will often be more identifiable. With the aim of making wealth more transparent a number of moves are being made at an international level particularly in relation to tax evasion and money laundering. The European Union (EU), Group of seven (G7) countries and the Bank for International Settlements (BIS), and not least the USA - one of the more aggressive pursuers of tax evaders and money launderers, are all contributing to making wealth much more transparent.

Whilst this might suggest that international wealth is becoming increasingly legitimate, it does not apply to all wealth and probably relates more to new wealth. There is little statistical evidence to prove that wealth is becoming more legitimate and perhaps it still will not be forthcoming in the near future. Rather, evidence will come more in the form of indirect measurement such as increased use of offshore services. For the old wealth, the alleged mountain of undeclared money that has built up worldwide over much of this century is likely to remain largely where it is.

Characteristics of an industry in change

One of the evident changes in international private banking is the central influence of the client that is now notable in connection with products, delivery, relationship management and service. Today's internationally minded client, particularly the more active business owner, is more informed about what is available in the marketplace, especially in the field of asset management, and can be seeking to invest in a range of markets and products involving higher levels of risk. Additionally, multiple provider relationships allow the client to compare service, product and performance, and to switch monies and dispense with providers after initial test periods.

People

Changes are identifiable within the areas of technical expertise, and of the remuneration, hiring and mobility of staff. In its current evolutionary stage, international private banking is firmly in the age of specialisation, reflecting the expansion of products and services to better match the requirements of the market. Fields of specialisation include commercial banking, investment banking such as corporate finance, tax, accountancy, law and investment management. All these specialist fields are highly relevant to international private banking, though the core areas remain banking and asset management together with the essential client skills.

In many ways, international private banking has gone through a cycle of professionalism in a number of areas including the important one of qualifications. Qualifications are numerous and relate principally to the area of advice-giving and technical competence. Professional qualifications are now *de rigeur* not least because of the increasing importance of the regulators, the monitoring of standards and the provider's reputation which is at stake.

In the past, private banking never really had the recruitment cachet that a merchant or investment bank might have had. However, now that it is one of the fastest-growing financial sectors, private banking is paying more and attracting a much high calibre of individual but facing a shortage of skilled individuals at all levels. Remuneration levels can depend on what the market will bear and whether the individual is well connected enough to generate significant new business rather than just manage a portfolio of clients.

There has been a change in compensation structure, typical of high-growth markets. Today, compensation for international private bankers, particularly those responsible for clients and new business, is typically a base salary with a high bonus proportion. Whilst there are strong similarities with compensation packages developed for investment banks because of the close organisational relationship some private banking providers have with banks, the level of remuneration for international private bankers is still reportedly some way behind that for investment bankers. Payment of bonuses is also sometimes phased beyond a one-year period to underpin employee loyalty and can consist of a number of elements including share options in the organisation. There is no doubt that international private banking is an increasingly performance-related business. Interestingly, remuneration is one of the more sensitive areas of the industry, and reveals cultural gaps and big differences in approach amongst providers.

Market presence and geographic dominance

A survey of market presence shows different approaches by international providers which can vary from a full service branch, offshore branch or representative office. Very few international private banking providers can be considered truly global, with most still reflecting their geographic specialisation and their own national origins. Only some of the US providers such as Citibank, Merrill Lynch and the three big Swiss commercial banks can truly be considered as providers on a global basis. The most widely represented are US providers: Citibank operates in 35 countries and Merrill Lynch has branches in 34. Expansion has been rapid and has been in tandem with consumer banking expansion in the case of Citibank and investment banking in the case of Merrill Lynch. It is expected that these providers will now focus on making returns on the expansion of outlets.

Although representation in markets has increased, the level of representation and depth of servicing available from these locations differ considerably, depending on the licence available from the regulatory authorities, the provider's appetite to commit permanent capital and resources, and the market desire for onshore/offshore servicing.

Providers typically cluster around a core set of client service locations (see Table 2.1). Most regions, except the Middle East, have seen significant expansion by providers trying to increase their coverage on the ground. Regions that have seen the most expansion have been Latin America and Asia. However, physical expansion has generally been a cautious affair, no doubt a throwback to the past when international private banking thrived on being out of sight.

Organisational structure[4]

Obfuscation (secrecy and discretion) has been characteristic of international private banking providers up until now. It could be construed that this has been perpetuated out of self-interest. In any event, this is now increasingly a past characteristic. Most of the main providers of international private banking services have recently undertaken some form of large-scale reorganisation designed to separate the private banking business line and give it greater organisational clarity and strength.

Citibank was one of the first providers to do this and created the Citibank Private Bank in 1994; two years later both Crédit Suisse and Swiss Bank Corporation changed their group operating structures and

Table 2.1 Regional representation of international private banks

Region	Core representation	Extended representation
Asia	Hong Kong Singapore	Bangkok, Jakarta, Manila, Taipei, Tokyo, Seoul
Europe	Zürich, Geneva London	Frankfurt, Madrid, Monte Carlo, Milan, Paris, Luxembourg, Vienna, Munich, Düsseldorf, Cannes, Athens
Latin America	Buenos Aires São Paolo Santiago Mexico City	Lima, Rio de Janeiro, Bogotá, Caracas
Middle East	Bahrain Dubai	Abu Dhabi
USA	New York Miami	Los Angeles, San Francisco

singled out private banking (among other business lines) as a clearly identifiable business line. Union Bank of Switzerland remains the significant exception to date but it must be only a matter of time before it follows suit. Others such as Coutts have always been only a private banking provider; however, it too has been part of an organisational change, coming much more tightly into the National Westminster fold to become part of a larger wealth-management group.

Given the opaque structures that providers have had to date, the new organisational structures are heralding an unprecedented new era of disclosure and transparency which also includes more detailed performance reporting, notably from the Swiss. The first important steps have been taken and performance of the private banking business line will come increasingly under the eyes of analysts looking at impact on shareholder return and making objective comparisons between the relative performances of private banking providers.

Information technology[5]

It has been estimated that costs relating to information technology (IT) account for, on average, 12% of private banking providers' expense base, the second highest cost behind people. To date, investment in IT has been concentrated in product systems such as portfolio management and operations in the back office. However, IT investment is now being made also in the front end, more specifically in client-management systems in recognition of the need to be more active and aggressive in both servicing and recruitment of clients.

Clients have been benefiting from technology developments in products, particularly the more sophisticated risk-management products that are now accessible to individuals, such as structured products. Delivery and servicing support are beginning to change and come under review too, thanks to the rapid rise in computer literacy and use of personal computers. Servicing support and delivery developments are evident in private banking in the growing number of web sites where information on non-interactive services is emerging. There will be increasing opportunities to diversity the servicing interface. Although the one-to-one relationship still remains central, the historical way of building relationships face to face might be supplemented by technology in the future.

Competition and the inflow of non-traditional providers such as brokers, investment banks and fund managers have forced the more traditional providers to expand their products and services, often in the advisory, trading and investment-management arena. In response to growing client awareness and demand for performance and investment return, providers are making product systems more responsive, allowing faster action in tune with market movements and changes in investment policy.

Service strategies are increasingly dependent on technology, the role of which spans the front office in a number of ways, including the development of client databases, the electronic storing of data such as Know Your Customer (KYC) data, office facilities and communication networks, particularly those linking the disparate parts of the organisation and supporting links between relationship managers and portfolio managers. One of the key advantages of developing front-office systems is that typically there are no legacy systems to deal with as there are in the back office. As usual, there is frequently the problem of having high expectations of costly information technology but not knowing how to use it to generate the desired results. To date the relationship management of clients is comparatively unsophisticated in terms of formal sales and service tools. The 'KYC' financial plan helps to develop a greater in-depth understanding of clients. However, other elements such as pro-active client programmes, with a composite client databank to hand, together with more exhaustive productivity data are not as commonplace as would be expected. Technology has a part to play in using segmentation more effectively, particularly in monitoring clients and evaluating services, costs, product development requirements and profitability. More sophisticated client segmentation would help providers that are pursuing total wealth management strategies.

The wealthy[6]

Growth of high net worth wealth has been universal across all regions. High net worth wealth has more than doubled in value during a decade, (see Chapter 1), reaching $16.6 trillion in 1996. Some of the significant factors behind wealth creation have been strong economic performance in general, the spectacular growth in Asia and the creation of new wealth. Although old wealth is clearly still the dominant proportion of wealth managed, the international private banking provider today has become much more focused and active in trying to gain a share of the new wealth.

The key factors are the shift of wealth from one generation to another and the new generation of wealth creators. The second generation and the new generation of wealth creators are often more sophisticated than their parents' generation, benefiting from education - often international education, and the increasing amount of information available about financial products, thanks to global media and technology.

It is also detectable that attitudes are beginning to change towards wealth management in a planned and more comprehensive way. Importantly, wealth creation and the inheritance of wealth are happening in a context of different risks and uncertainties from those of the past. Changes are noted in client's attitudes towards taxation, planning over a longer term, return on investment, risk profile of products, confidentiality and inheritance.

Key segments

In the past, with a highly specialised service designed for individuals looking for asset protection, the wealthy typically self-selected the type of service they required. With a much larger and diverse market, the needs of the wealthy are becoming more disparate and segmentation is now important. Self-selection does still play a part but, the choice for clients is much greater and, for providers, the dynamics of servicing the increasing number of client types are more complex. It is therefore important to segment the client base and focus on those segments that are the most attractive in terms of capabilities required and returns achievable.

A number of key segments have emerged that can be characterised as follows:

Wealth preservers: Often considered the bedrock of international private banking, where the older generation can be more risk averse and conservative in their approach to their wealth and where the very wealthy are not solely motivated by capital appreciation.

Wealth developers: Described as such because they are often first-generation entrepreneurs who are typical of high net worth individuals today, starting up their businesses in a more liberal and capitalistic economic environment.

Wealth builders: Often heirs of the older generation of entrepreneurs who are taking over the reins of established family businesses; foreign educated and more worldly wise and skilled to take the business forward.

Wealth concealers: Their primary motivation is to ensure total secrecy regarding their wealth; typically politicians and individuals involved in illegal activities.

Wealth dynasties: Possessing extremely high levels of wealth. Often these wealthy families have a full-time office looking after their affairs and co-ordinating the professionals.

Wealth developers and builders typify the new generation of wealth creators and are considered the fastest growing segments in the international private banking marketplace.

Segmentation attempts by private banking providers are generally unsophisticated, reflecting the immaturity of the market and the recent emergence of newer wealth. Criteria used are simple and typically they might relate to geography, ethnic origin of client, attitude to risk, source of funds, level of investible assets and whether the client is managed on a discretionary or advisory basis. However, there are important exclusions, with some providers being wary of certain wealth concealers from various countries.

Key changes in high net worth needs

Changes in the needs of high net worth individuals seldom happen overnight but instead emerge slowly as the generational shift takes place and the effect of external forces is felt. Some of the more significant attitudes that private bankers have identified as changing are those that relate to financial planning, active management and performance.

Financial planning

There have been a number of barriers, particularly in the past, which have discouraged international private banking providers from assisting clients to manage their financial affairs on a more planned basis. These barriers have been wide ranging, but one of them is where a client's demands are very limited either with a very short-term focus or extending only to asset protection. There have been other inhibiting factors that are more culturally based, such as the use of trusts and legal structures that make financial planning quite difficult to achieve in some markets.

Importantly, with a shift in generation comes a change in attitude, particularly among the heirs of significant wealth. Changes in attitude include those regarding the risk-and-reward equation of tax evasion and the infringement of regulations; often, the option of legitimate tax planning is chosen. Other factors at play are the future payment of inheritance taxes and estate duties that on the face of it can sometimes mean a significant loss of wealth by heirs. Refinancing and restructuring family businesses can be the preferred routes and these solutions are sometimes seen more clearly by the second generation.

Active management

There is considerable evidence that management is becoming more active. The profile of an international private banking client is differing from the past, particularly in terms of age, lifestyle and education. The increased sophistication means a growing demand for information, higher-risk products and control of financial affairs.

The growing sophistication of high net worth individuals is reinforced by changes in the providers' services: products and services have expanded particularly the more complex and technical advisory products; servicing structures have changed to accommodate the more demanding client; and there are moves towards more onshore servicing with the aim of getting closer to the client.

Performance

In line with growing sophistication is the heightened awareness of performance among international private banking clients. This undoubtedly has been fuelled by the huge amounts of published information and data on the financial markets, now freely available, as well as the growing competition. Other factors driving changes in pricing and products are the low interest rate and low inflation environment in Europe and the USA. But there is still variation in what constitutes good (and not so good) performance. The underlying trend is that passive or ineffectual relationship management is increasingly exposed. However, dissatisfaction can be caused as much by performance expectations as actual performance. Either way, this is a complex issue. What clouds performance is how it is judged and this can be done in a number of ways:

- Nominal growth rather than real growth.
- Performance against a number of different benchmarks ranging from a high-interest deposit account and stock market indices and other stock markets especially the client's domestic stock market.
- Absolute performance.
- Assessment against other providers.
- Assessment against client's own achievements with other investments e.g. real estate and own business.

A number of other changes underpin the focus on performance by providers, as follows:

- 'Beauty parades' in the provider selection process and the use of multiple providers have become more common features of the private banking industry.
- Increased reporting on products, both in terms of depth of information provided and frequency of reporting through integrated statements.
- Publishing of performance measured against benchmarks to assist understanding of in-house performance.
- Clearer establishment of client's own benchmark of performance timeframe and of base or reference currency.

Providers – dynamics and dimensions

The intensity of competition is not a matter of just number of competitors but also type of provider, and the dynamics within international private banking reflect both factors. Whereas at one time the market choice was only between privately owned banks and commercial banks, the industry now consists of a much more extensive array of providers. Provider origins still matter because they influence the culture of the provider as well as its particular strengths and emphases. To the advantage of the providers, and especially the new ones, the fragmented and sizeable nature of the market means that there are many ways in which to compete.

The main provider types include.

- **Privately owned banks:** Most often these are Swiss. Identified strengths are their partnership structure which fosters employee loyalty, and the fact that culturally they have remained true to their roots, providing superior and individually tailored service to their customers. Their limitations today are generally those relating to product range, ability to lend and international presence. Product shortfalls have been remedied through alliances with other product providers such as fund management houses and by diversifying into institutional fund management.
- **Commercial banks:** Mostly European and US banks which are multinational but with a strong home base. Some have strong historical ties to markets such as the Middle East, Asia and Latin America which has helped them in their pursuit of new markets. Many of these commercial banks have become universal providers with extensive investment capability.
- **Investment banks:** Mostly US with specialist skills appropriate for very wealthy clients. Skills relate to investment management and to privately owned businesses; services might include raising capital and bringing the businesses to the market.
- **Brokers:** Strong advisory and execution capability combined with access to diverse investment research.
- **Asset managers:** Investment product specialists with limited distribution and narrow product range, appropriate for clients looking for a more integrated wealth management approach.

Table 2.2 Key international private banking providers and private client assets 1995/96

Estimated amount of assets (US $ billion)	Provider
> 300	Union Bank of Switzerland, Swiss Bank Corporation
> 200	Crédit Suisse
> 125	Chase Manhattan Bank
> 95	Citibank Bank
30–50	Merrill Lynch, HSBC, JP Morgan, Dresdner Bank, Deutsche Bank
20–30	ABN Amro, Coutts, Barclays, Banque Nationale de Paris, Lloyds, Banque Indosuez
< 20	Safra Suisse, Bank J Vontobel, Bank Julius Baer

Strengths are their diversity of fund products and the possibility of comparing performance.

Industry dominance[7]

To date, industry dominance seems to be largely measured by client assets although this is not the only measure of success and is not necessarily a true measure. Size though is an indication of strength. Individual statistics on providers are rarely provided but, various estimates have been made and these together with some recently published data by a few providers themselves have been used for compiling Table 2.2. Comparing like with like is problematic, with definitions varying and institutional monies combined in some cases.

Some of the larger Swiss privately owned banks are those that are part of the Geneva Group of Private Bankers: Pictet, Lombard Odier, Mirabaud, Darier Hentsch and Bordier (see Fig. 2.3). Institutional and private client assets are combined for reporting purposes.

Strategies[8]

International private banking strategies typically revolve around product leadership, brand identification and service quality.

- **Product leadership:** A strategy of product leadership would aim at a combination of depth, breadth, innovation, price competitiveness, technological support and performance.

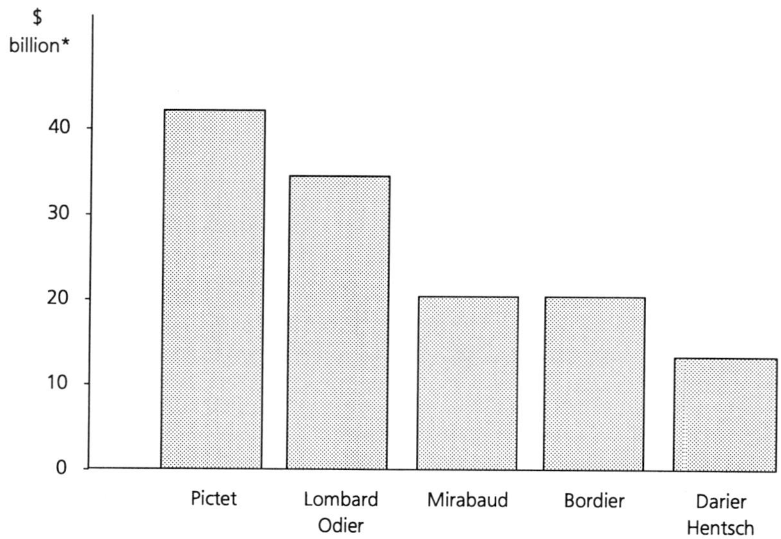

Figure 2.3 Assets of institutional and private clients of Swiss privately owned banks 1995/96.

* converted from Swiss francs at prevailing rates.

Source: The Wernlin Directory, 1995/1996, Private Banking, Asset Management in Switzerland, Gunter Woernle.

- **Brand identification:** Branding is a combination of organisational history and culture, individual and type of client services, awareness and reputation.
- **Service quality:** The pursuit of a service quality strategy involves paying attention to the correct service priorities, quality of staff, information technology, and having a client-focused culture.

In addition, providers undertake what have been described as significant one-off actions in order to compete.

In the more developed markets such as those in Europe and the USA, local competition is often strong and tends to dominate the selection; this means foreign banks have a difficult time gaining market share and are confined to niche markets. Where institutions are particularly successful in their home market and where competition is reaching saturation point, the trend is to seek international markets. The European and US providers tend to pursue opportunities in Asia and Latin America. Other corporate strategies such as consumer banking and investment banking often influence how the private banking business sector grows, given the market and business synergies, and they often expand together. All in all, international private banking strategies so far have a touch of the herd-like quality about them.

Product leadership

The traditional model of international private banking is associated with discretionary and non-discretionary portfolio management and certain offshore services. Although these are still central to international private banking, the development of products and services has been based on a combination of expansion and change in emphasis as market demand and new products come on stream. Additionally, products and services reflect organisational origins and strengths. Today, providers typically offer a much more highly developed service proposition, designed for a more discerning and more segmented market.

Notable too is a shift across providers towards a middle ground between product excellence and service excellence. Providers have generally started to develop a more integrated approach to providing wealth management services, recognising the value and strength of retaining relationships over the long terms supported by tailored cross-selling programmes.

Product leadership is multidimensional. Where the product leader is distinctive is in the breadth and depth of its product range and its ability to offer innovative products, often through in-house capacity. Typically, product leaders are leaders across a range of products and services. Citibank is often quoted as a product leader for the breadth and depth of its product range and for its development of innovative products. The issue for providers trying to gain (or even protect) market share is how much to expand their products and services given the diversity of competition and in some senses the ill-defined nature of private banking services. Some of the more typical exclusions are: banking services where the provider is not a commercial bank; unsecured lending or lending against illiquid assets; and tax and specialised services such as real estate and art advisory services.

Key areas of product and service expansion have been:

- **Investment funds:** Breadth and depth of funds available differ from provider to provider. Extremes are found, from extensive in-house choice to branded funds from specialised investment houses. Some providers will also offer third party investment products as a matter of course.

- **Advisory services:** Where clients are active and sophisticated in their financial knowledge with a strong desire to have control and management of their wealth, advisory services have expanded to meet this demand. Private bankers add value by providing data and investment research and translating these into tailored investment opportunities for the client. Research capability can be key here.
- **Offshore services:** The larger providers in particular have expanded their presence to a number of core jurisdictions which allows them to provide a more extended range of offshore services, particularly those relating to tax planning. Increasingly important product and service areas are trusts and legal structures.
- **Structured and specialist products:** Given the scale of private wealth, individuals now have access to structured products such as derivatives. In addition, clients can be provided with highly selective investment opportunities in private placements and special-purpose funds.

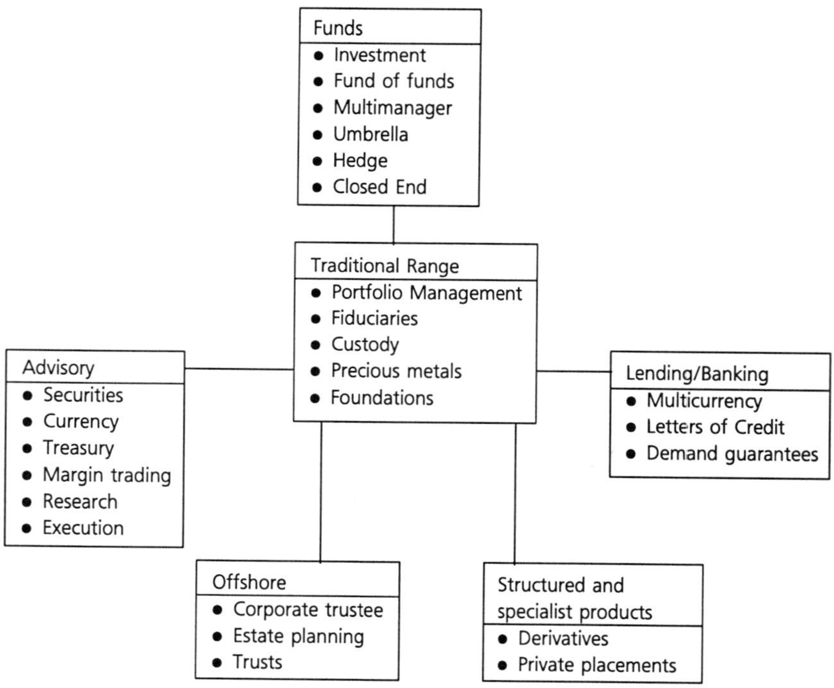

Figure 2.4 Developments in international private banking products and services.

- **Lending services:** These are typically provided on a secured basis and include multi-currency facilities, letters of credit and demand guarantees.
- **Other services:** Not so commonly found but still available are advisory services relating to highly specialised areas such as art.

Further developments are expected in pensions and insurance products. Other important facets of products and services are the ability to co-ordinate services such as those provided through the investment bank or corporate banking arm. However, the core range of products and services will continue to centre on investment and tax planning products and services. This emphasis on technical and advisory-based products begs the question of the provider's ability to handle such a breadth and depth of product range and how tenable the role of the single-relationship manager is.

Pricing policies are diverse and hard to compare. Overall, pricing is becoming increasingly transparent and practices have changed, with the Swiss ending their pricing cartel in 1990 and now the increasing availability of published material on charges, helping competitors and clients alike to make comparisons. Essentially, the prices reflect the product and service combinations of interest spread, fees and transaction-based charges. In discretionary investment management, for example, two types of pricing systems exist: an all-in-one fee charged annually or six-monthly, and a number of separate fees covering the management, brokerage, custody, and miscellaneous activities and stamp duty. Pricing differs between centres and comparisons between the centres of London and Switzerland reveal that UK providers generally have higher management fees but have larger volume discounts and lower brokerage fees and stamp duties.

Luckily for providers, private banking has the distinction of serving clients who generally are happy to pay a premium on the basis of a value-added service. Price sensitivity alone is not typically an issue and neither are international private banking providers selected on their price competitiveness alone. However, pricing does become important in the value-for-money equation and is sometimes cited when value for money is not received and the client departs.

Brand identification[9]

Private banking is the one of the few remaining financial services – arguably the only one – where brand values are important and where cachet, however it is defined, still matters. For international private banking, brand values are all about reputation, value and quality.

Of all the international private banking providers, perhaps Citibank has the most recognised brand name worldwide. Citicorp, in particular, understands the value of a well-respected brand name and has openly stated that it is striving to create the world's most respected branded image for banking services. What is more, it is Citicorp's belief that brand equity translates into meaningful and measurable value for stockholders. Evidence of success as a global name came to Citibank when in 1995, it was ranked sixth (113 places ahead of its nearest rival financial services firm) among leading companies in Asia, which included Coca-Cola and Microsoft.

A change from the past is the promotion of the brand and the role of advertising and other promotional tools is becoming increasingly important. Whereas once discretion and a low profile were considered the only way to do business, now providers are taking on more overt market positions and raising their profile with both existing and potential clients. Recent positioning statements in corporate awareness campaigns have included:

- **Citibank** — "The Citi that never sleeps"
- **Union Bank of Switzerland** — "*The* Bank"
- **Crédit Suisse Private Banking** — "Sets the standard for international private banking and investment management"
- **JP Morgan** — "Morgan Means More"
- **Julius Baer** — "Fine Art of Swiss Private Banking"
- **Geneva's Private Bankers** — "People say we are too high-principled. But where would your investments be without principles?"

Much of this has to do with building a global brand and recognising that competition is growing. However, advertising will still remain only a small part of how international private banking providers do business, given that it is a niche market and this means of reaching clients is potentially expensive.

However, the importance of the name counts for a lot and an

indication of parentage too carries weight. A number of branding techniques are used:

- **Umbrella brand:** HSBC Private Banking is the umbrella brand name for a number of providers which still retain different international operating brands, sometimes confusingly, such as British Bank of the Middle East (BBME) and Midland Private Banking International. This stems from the corporate view that local names are still considered important and is typical of the federal style of HSBC.
- **Sub-brand of the parent brand:** Citibank Private Bank is a sub-brand of Citicorp and in a similar vein there are Lloyds Private Banking and Barclays Private Bank showing clear and strong relationship with the parent.
- **Independent brand of the parent:** Retention of the old family name is common in international private banking. A string of Swiss privately owned banks acquired by the three large Swiss commercial banks still operate under a separate brand name e.g. Bank Leu, Bank Clariden, Bank Hoffman, Cantrade Private Bank, Armand von Ernst, Bank Ehinger, Adler and Ferrier Lullin. Coutts, owned by National Westminster Bank, continues to maintain its original name.
- **Associated branding:** The five largest of the Swiss partnerships promote themselves as a single body. Pictet, Lombard Odier, Darier Hentsch, Bordier and Mirabaud co-operate within the Group of Geneva's Private Bankers (Groupement des Banquiers Privés Genevois).

For a client, strength of a brand has a lot to do with cultural affinity and nationality. The US brand names typically suggest longevity and universality. Conversely, the Swiss brand names stand for heritage, confidentiality and a certain style of service. However, reputation cuts a number of ways and there are several less positive features connected not so much with the provider but with the financial centres with which providers are associated.

- Switzerland has a mixed reputation, not least for its position on banking confidentiality but, more recently, for the issue of Jewish wealth deposited during the Second World War. Although the inquest into events may not affect actual inflows of wealth to Swiss banks, despite some rallying calls to Jews worldwide, these events must add a slight tarnish to Switzerland's overall image, and they are far from over. A report issued by the US government suggests that some Swiss banks after the War continued to thwart the course of justice. The report also throws into question a number of other countries that were neutral during the War.

- The US brand can be less attractive when clients are concerned about confidentiality and about the role and strength of the Inland Revenue Services (IRS) in ensuring that taxes are paid.

Organisational origins can also influence perception. Merrill Lynch is a good example of this; its origins as a commission-driven broker have played against it in establishing itself as a serious international private banking provider. Changing market perceptions takes time and for Merrill this has involved a number of deep-set changes such as expansion of product range, moving to a relationship-management approach, building full service branches and recruiting private bankers and other product specialists; thereby breaking the broker mould.

Service quality

All providers will say they are striving to give their clients the best possible service. How this is achieved differs from one provider to another. Some of the keys are structure, culture and delivery strategy.

In the past, international private banking was often an ancillary service under the management of the overall country manager. Now that it is of greater strategic importance and operates more often as a clearly defined and separate line of business, its structure within private banks has been remodelled. Private banking structures are now typically centred on the client, ensuring a clear focus on roles and responsibilities. The remodelling also makes services much harder to replicate competitively, given the lead times needed for effecting such changes. Changes in structure have been deeply felt by private banking providers, particularly the more traditional ones where a strong sense of history has maintained the *status quo*. However, the changes indicate a clear recognition that the practices of the past are no longer tenable. A number of structures have evolved from the traditional servicing model, each combining a variation of the core elements of relationship management, portfolio management, fund management, research and investment strategy. In support of the improved structures, other changes have been made concerning, for example, back-office systems' investment, standardised portfolios, centralising of portfolio management, and centralising of research

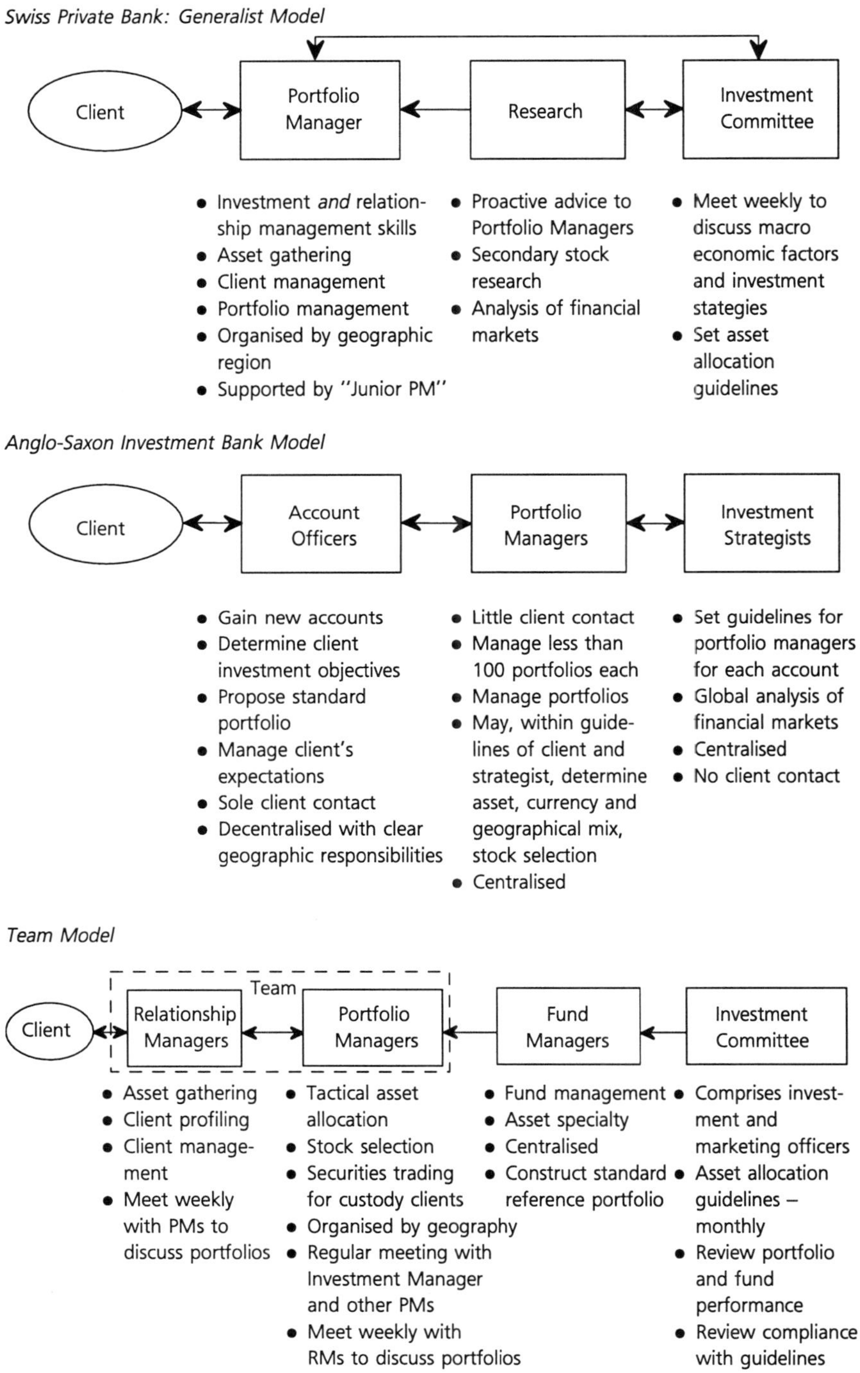

Figure 2.5 Different servicing models in international private banking.

Source: Gemini Consulting

and investment strategy guidelines which cover asset allocation, currency and geographical mix and stock selection. The benefits of the changes are greater focus on clients, investment performance and investment management.

Another aspect of service strategy is culture. Historically, private banking services provided from Europe reflected the dominance of the Swiss, hence the evolution of the Swiss style of private banking and the investment orientation. The Swiss style of private banking has long been considered a service to emulate. However, it is sometimes hard to define as many people - especially the Swiss themselves - suggest that there is more to private banking than service and products.

Aspects of culture, ethics and style are all pat of its uniqueness. Its definition depends on who is asked and even then the answer may still not be clear. With a hint of superiority, it has been said that private banking from Switzerland is inimitable in the same way that a Ferrari can be built only in Italy. Once experienced never forgotten, perhaps. Interestingly, a parallel proposition is developing in Asia where private bankers in that region refer to the Asian style of private banking as a distinctive way of servicing the region's wealthy. Like the Swiss style, its evolution is firmly rooted in the culture of the region. Its distinctiveness is due to high levels of personal service and attention to detail together with product know-how and strong technology interface. In a comparative sense, the Asian style reflects the much more active and performance-oriented profile of today's clients than the more conservative and traditional client of a Swiss private bank in the past.

One of the major departures in service strategies has been the pursuit of an onshore servicing programme in the clear belief that certain services are better delivered locally and that relationship building can be better achieved with greater physical presence. The onshore and offshore servicing issue is not entirely clear cut, but these providers will argue that by having an onshore option, a competitive position over the long term is established, as well as a choice of servicing location where neither the private banker or the client are disadvantaged. For those few providers, such as Merrill Lynch and Citibank, that have established onshore servicing, the issue is about giving clients a choice, and most competitors cannot offer this, while some are still firmly camped in the historical way of servicing remotely.

With wealth flows and client servicing preference transcending geographical boundaries and organisational structures, establishing operating guidelines can be a challenge for international private banking providers. The key areas are those of marketing and servicing effort, and recognition. Increased global co-ordination is an important issue for some providers, particularly the larger ones, especially where two centres seek new clients from the same market and where the client wants to be served. Generally, more radical approaches to co-ordinating the business effort and to eliminating any parochial tensions need to be found throughout the industry. In the case of Merrill Lynch, a solution has been found by increasingly organising the business around markets not offices. In important markets, a market leader is appointed to orchestrate the prospecting activity of private bankers from a number of offices. The market leader is compensated for new business generation in the market irrespective of which office books the business.

The private banker might have to co-ordinate products and services from within the organisation, which might be located elsewhere from the relationship manager. Some issues are highly practical, such as knowing whom to contact. Others require investment, for example the technology needed for a global communication network such as that which operates within Citibank.

One-off actions[10]

Not surprisingly, there have been a number of one-off actions undertaken by providers to change their competitive footing in the international private banking marketplace. Acquisitions are still comparatively rare and have the potential to bring benefits of market share and market know-how, provided the staff and the clients are retained. In the past, acquisitions were largely confined to home markets, as for example in Switzerland, where a string of independent private banks was acquired by the large commercial banks. In contrast, acquisitions at group level have provided parent companies with an expanded private banking line of business as in the case of the more recent acquisition by HSBC Holdings of Midland Bank in the UK and Dresdner Bank's acquisition of the UK merchant bank, Kleinwort Benson. In the case of HSBC, Midland Bank had operations in London and Switzerland in the form of Midland Private Banking International and Guyerzeller Bank. For Kleinwort Benson, market penetration in the Middle East in particular has given Dresdner Bank a well-established foothold. Acquisitions, though, can also bring potential problems of integration and the reaction of clients to being acquired by a different institution.

From the seller's perspective, given the stead inflow of competition, it begs the question of why sell? Reasons largely relate to focus and future strategy. Standard Chartered's sale of its private banking portfolio to Swiss Bank Corporation caught the market a little by surprise, given that Standard Chartered is a leading foreign bank in Asia and was considered by the competition as a strong and successful force in private banking. Although acquisitions are rare to date in international private banking, there was apparently no shortage of bidders. It was not the only acquisition made in 1996 by Swiss Bank Corporation: it also bought a private banking portfolio of Chase Manhattan Bank, consisting largely of Latin American clients. Reasons for the sale by Chase were attributed to focus and the move to maintain a higher threshold of assets from clients.

Where acquisitions are not forthcoming, alliances and joint ventures are becoming increasingly evident particularly among the medium to small providers. To date, these have involved domestic and international providers seeking to gain footholds in the international private banking business and new markets such as in Asia and the expected opening up of South Africa.

Wealth destinations for cross-border wealth[11]

It was only in the 1960s that offshore financial centres started to emerge more visibly and to play a more global role. Today, the number continues to grow and it has been estimated that there are over 50 offshore centres, although only about half would be considered fully developed. Centres have relative strengths and selection of centre is made by provider and by client. From a provider's perspective the selection hangs on a number of criteria such as reputation, regulatory environment and nature of jurisdiction, cost and quality of staff available. For a client, selection can be a question of preference for a particular centre, based on geographic and cultural considerations; desire for complete anonymity, or need for tax avoidance and asset protection. Each centre will offer a particular strength to meet one or other of these requirements.

A significant factor relates to the different legal structures that can be set up across jurisdictions, particularly where there is a need for tax planning. Larger providers have more recently expanded to ensure that they can provide legal structures from both common law and civil law jurisdictions. This means greater choice for the client when it comes to tax efficiency, control of assets, confidentiality, costs to set up and maintain structures and affinity with a particular location (see Table 2.3).

Overall, the selection of financial centre is not necessarily a question

Table 2.3 Summary of funds flow 1996

Source of wealth	Destination profile
Europe	Wealth often stays within Europe where some of the most important worldwide centres are located such as Zürich, Geneva, Luxembourg, London and the Channel Islands.
Asia	Wealth typically has a strong regional attachment to Asia and local stock markets and to real estate and business investment. However, wealth also avidly follows attractive investment opportunities worldwide and family members who have emigrated. Typical destinations are London and the Channel Islands.
Latin America	Wealth has a strong attachment to client's local market with strong preference shown for the USA and US dollar-denominated investments. With an emerging appetite for tax planning, proportions of wealth are held in Europe, particularly the Channel Islands and Switzerland.
Middle East	Wealth is held in Switzerland and the more performance-oriented centres of London and New York.
USA	Wealth often flows to Caribbean destinations such as the Cayman Islands, and to London and Switzerland.

of selecting only a single centre. The internationally wealthy wherever they are resident will very often have monies in a number of centres, typically with several providers, the choice of centres and providers reflecting business, personal and lifestyle preferences. Though hard to measure, industry estimates suggest an increasing level of cross-border wealth together with a short list of financial centres through which this wealth is managed, reflecting a move away from the traditional safe haven of Switzerland.

Assets held offshore have grown significantly largely because of the growing trend of international diversification and the relaxation of currency controls. Where once Switzerland was the single most important centre for international private banking, competition has hotted up between centres. However, Switzerland remains the dominant and largest asset manager of cross-border wealth (see Chapter 4), half of which is reputedly in the hands of the three large Swiss commercial banks. The Channel Islands, Dublin and Singapore are viewed as centres which will grow in importance over the next five years, with Hong Kong and Luxembourg becoming less important, given the growth of Singapore and Dublin respectively.

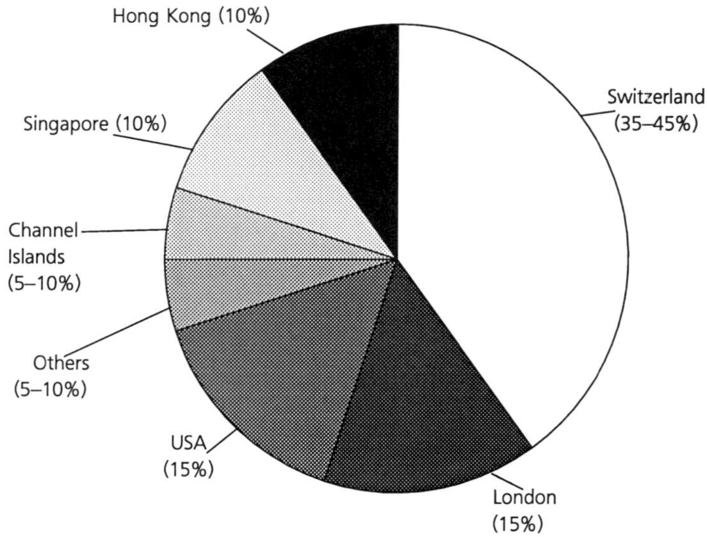

Figure 2.6 Estimated cross-border assets managed by financial centres.
Source: Crédit Suisse First Boston, January 1996.

Regulation and legislation[12]

Undoubtedly, it is regulation and legislation at both national and international level which provide some of the most important parameters in which providers and wealthy individuals alike can mange wealth. The international private banking providers have to operate in markets that are diverse in their regulations as well as conform to multiple sets of regulations. Looking ahead, it is likely that with authorities worldwide increasingly keen on enforcement, the trend is for more not less regulation. Key areas continue to be banking confidentiality, cross-border co-operation to combat money laundering, and unfair tax competition between jurisdictions.

Banking confidentiality

One of the major curiosities about private banking is that as an industry it spans a peculiar divide of service and secrecy. Whilst the term private banking on the one hand can conjure up images of sophisticated financial services to the wealthy citizens of the world, it also has strong associations with illegal activities, money laundering, sunny locations and shady individuals. Undoubtedly, it is the contract of confidentiality between bank and customer that is a major contributing factor to this image. However, the need for financial secrecy will continue to be a significant contributor to the growth of funds offshore. The crux of the matter is the legitimacy of the wealth and the degree of protection provided through duties of confidentiality between provider and customer.

Money that is motivated by financial secrecy falls into three categories:

- **Money where the beneficial owner is legitimately protected by anonymity.** Protection is offered by trusts and corporate structures where tax planning and legitimate tax avoidance are required.
- **Money that is evading local tax liabilities.** This is where tax evasion is the illegal non-payment of taxes either by under-declaring income or by over-declaring deductions or exemptions in the country of residency for tax purposes, usually in the face of civil or criminal penalty.
- **Dirty money.** This is where monies are obtained through illegal activities such as drug-dealing, terrorism, smuggling, political theft and so on.

Whether to a domestic or an international private banking client, the duty of banking confidentiality applies. Although not exclusively an issue for the international arena, this duty becomes particularly important where wealth crosses borders. The duty of confidentiality varies across jurisdictions, some of which even boast of the robustness of the protection afforded to clients. It is undoubtedly in relation to Switzerland and its banking laws that this is one of the more enduring topics in the private banking industry. However, as international co-operation and standards on confidentiality increase, there does appear to be a decisive change in attitude towards confidentiality within high net worth individuals, and private bankers are beginning to express the view that confidentiality is now somewhat overrated as a major reason for a centre or a provider being selected.

International private banking providers are managing monies for legitimate tax planning and, allegedly, also monies that are undeclared. They are not legally responsible for the payment of their clients' personal taxes, but reputable providers normally shun monies obtained from criminal activities, by insisting on knowing identity of the beneficial owner of the wealth. In the case of many institutions

Table 2.4 Wealth held by eight high-profile individuals

Haile Selaisse	$15 billion of foreign assets at time of death in 1975. Was also making regular deposits of gold.[1]
Ex-president Marcos	$5-10 billion laundered through Hong Kong.[1] Extensive fortune elsewhere, which The Philippines government is trying to take back.
Anastasio Somoza	Supposed to have exported $500 million from Nicaragua before his overthrow in 1979.[1]
'Baby Doc' Duvalier	Reportedly stashed away $200–500 million 1971 and 1986.[1]
Saddam Hussein	Allegedly deposited $51 million in a major Swiss bank in Geneva in 1972. It is believed that he controls funds of $32 billion.[2]
Erich Honecker	$260 million moved out of East Germany through Bank Austria.[3]
Raul Salinas	Brother of former Mexican President Carlos Salinas de Gortari, reported to have shifted some $120 million from Mexico to Switzerland.[4]
Captain Yaya Jammeh	President of The Gambia, reported to have deposited over $20 million in accounts, including one with Crédit Lyonnais in Geneva.[5]

Notes

[1]Ingo Walter, *Secret Money*, pp. 71–72; [2]Jeffrey Robinson, *The Laundreymen*; [3]Jeffrey Robinson, op.cit.; [4]'A $15 trillion piggy bank', *Business Week*, 24 June 1996, p. 62; [5]'A Swiss fondu', *The Economist*, 18 January 1997, p. 46.

cash is not acceptable, extensive checks are done to identify the true origins of the wealth and indeed, wealth from certain countries is considered off limits. All big banks have tightened up procedures for taking on new clients to avoid 'black' or illegitimate wealth.

Whether private banks like it or not, they are bound to be tainted by the problem of local tax evasion and dirty money because it is financial institutions which supply the products by which this money can be moved. It also does not help the reputation of private banks that, in the not-so-distant past, private bankers were characterised as 'carpet baggers', so called because of the alleged meetings with clients and the handing over of cash in suitcases. Furthermore, high profile attention has been given to services rendered to politicians and their associates who have found monetary refuge, particularly in Switzerland (see Table 2.4).

Cross-border co-operation to combat money laundering

For the law enforcement bodies, banking confidentiality can harbour illegal activities even though the individuals involved risk financial penalties and imprisonment. The decision to cross borders illegally is arrived at after weighing up the risk and the rewards. The attraction, of course, is the expectation that the long arm of the law will find it difficult to penetrate other jurisdictions once the national boundary has been crossed. Despite increasing levels of international co-operation, this undoubtedly remains all too much the case.

The issue of banking confidentiality, the protection it allegedly affords the money launderers and tax evaders, and the profits derived for the so-called customer and the institutions involved, are a cause for major concern for the law enforcement agencies in all jurisdictions and continue to be high on the international agenda. It has been estimated that laundered wealth is the third-largest global business after foreign exchange and petroleum. Even about ten years ago, the underground economy was estimated at 7–10% of GDP in most industrialised economies.

International co-operation has grown as a result of the increasing difficulties faced by national law enforcement bodies once criminally derived monies have entered the international financial system. Key components of this co-operation have been:

- The Basle Statement of Principles, issued in 1988, which articulates a number of operating principles aimed at denying the banking system to those involved in money laundering.
- The 1988 Vienna Convention which demanded that drug money laundering be made a criminal offence and that banking secrecy be curbed if an obstacle to legal investigation.
- In 1989, the 'Group of 7' countries formed the Financial Action Task Force (FATF). Out of this came a blueprint with 40 measures. Although most governments have put in place anti-money-laundering laws, none has fully adopted all the measures.
- European Union (EU) Directive on Money Laundering and Offshore Centres (91/308) was built on the Basle Statement of Principles and aims to harmonise member states' laundering laws. The directive includes not just member states but also the other members of the European Economic Area Agreement. Most of Europe's offshore financial centres have yet to implement the directive. However, Guernsey, Jersey and the Isle of Man are expected to conform fully with FATF's blueprint by the end of 1997.

Advanced technology and the globalisation of the financial markets have unquestionably added to the uphill struggle to detect and stem illegitimate wealth flows. The USA has been instrumental in the battle against dirty money, but there is no single consistent international approach to the problem. Tensions exist between governments and banks as to respective roles and responsibilities. Moreover, there are countervailing forces to the global tide. While banking confidentiality may well have been undermined by certain national government actions, at the same time, in other parts of the world, money with dubious origins appears to be welcomed. Seychelles, for instance, was planning to introduce a new law whereby anyone depositing $10 million or more was immune from prosecution by foreign police forces. However, international pressure has forced the government of the Seychelles to shelve this. Advertisements are also found in the international media offering specific help in avoiding Big Brother's tax net; anonymous banking and transferring of cash without paper trails provide wealthy individuals with another source of help to manage their wealth internationally. In some ways, this is another world from international private banking, in others, these activities are distant cousins. Some would agree that offshore centres have no place in the contemporary Western banking system.

Unfair tax competition

The OECD has set up a task force (announced February 1997) to look into tax competition in the belief that internationally mobile funds are tax driven and that they harm domestic country revenues. Special tax regimes have been cited as potentially harming revenues from other countries. The task force project will:

- Identify the impact of tax competition and what constitutes fair and harmful tax competition.
- Review how tax competition is addressed today and whether measures adopted are effective against harmful tax competition.
- Recommend ways in which governments either individually or collectively can improve their positions against negative tax competition.

Key considerations are the degree to which tax rates are lower for internationally mobile funds compared with domestic investment; to what extent tax incentives are offered to affect location decision; the time limit applied on the benefits; and whether there is no clear economic objective for the tax regime. Non-OECD countries including tax havens will be covered by the survey as well as preferential tax regimes in member states such as the Irish Republic, Belgium and the Netherlands.

In addition, the EU is set to tackle taxation (again). Little has been achieved to date with regard to harmonisation of taxation except with Value-Added Tax (VAT) which has parameters within which rates are set. However, in the context of progress towards a single currency, certain countries such as France, Germany, Italy and Belgium regard diverging tax rates across Europe as too costly for their domestic economies. It has been estimated that Luxembourg costs Germany as much as $12 billion in annual tax revenues by attracting German funds across the border with its lack of withholding tax. The aim is to produce a code of good conduct. However, unanimity is expected to be hard to achieve.

Profitability[13]

A number of factors reinforce the overall optimism within the international private banking industry. Key elements such as the high returns on capital, high levels of profitability and its relatively stable income streams are some of the reasons why private banking has been attracting such an inflow of new providers. Underpinning the inflow is the private bankers' optimism with regard to future profitability. Predictions have been made that overall revenue growth rates will be in excess of 11% over the next five years, despite the fact that there is a core of private banks underperforming which are because of low revenue growth, loss of clients and of staff, and high operating cost bases.

A number of factors reinforce the overall optimism:

- **Market growth rates:** High net worth assets are expected to continue to grow fast and approach $25 trillion by the year 2000, which would represent a 45% increase on the 1996 total. Furthermore, estimates of past growth of the size of cross-border wealth together with other aspects of market behaviour such as growing use of international tax planning tools and international equities suggest enough reasons to be optimistic about the growing size of the international private banking market place.

- **Growing focus on new clients:** Market growth is reflected in the expected shifts towards new clients. Proportionately, new clients are becoming more important to providers with their revenue contribution growing and overtaking that of existing clients.

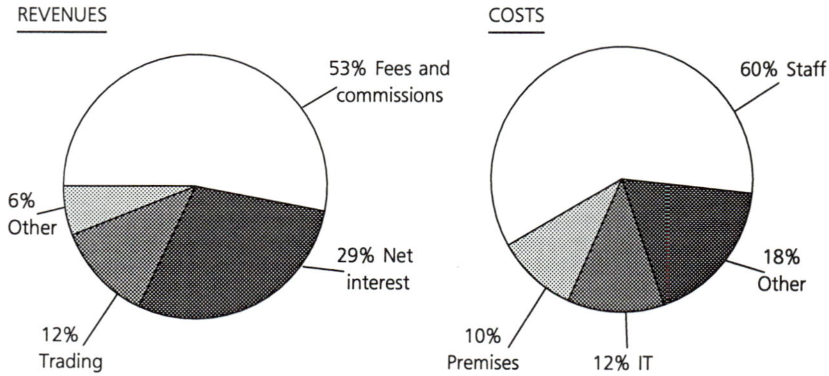

Figure 2.7 Current average revenue and cost distribution of private banking providers.
Source: Price Waterhouse European Private Banking Survey 1996/97.

- **Relative attractiveness of margins.** Like domestic private banking, margins will remain relatively attractive and international private banking will continue to be one of the last remaining businesses where fees and margins are so attractive, notwithstanding growing competition and greater scrutiny by clients as to what the provider is offering and the value for money that the service represents (see Fig. 2.7). Average management fees vary between centres but have been estimated as high as 103 basis points in the UK and 51 basis points in Switzerland (1996). These have increased significantly from 1990 estimates.
- **One-off investment costs.** Investment for the future is still evident among all providers, with provisions for restructuring, hiring of more staff, and investment in technology has and will be affecting bottom-line performance over a number of years.

Although it has been common practice for US and some of the European providers to publish performance results, it is significant that it was only in 1996 that the major Swiss providers took the first step towards performance reporting. Importantly, this now gives the opportunity to compare relative performances and understand more clearly where shareholder value is achieved and the part that private banking results play in the overall portfolio of a financial services group. This in turn will provoke greater competition as the financial bench marks become more transparent. Many of the important private banking providers have been through reorganisation changes and in

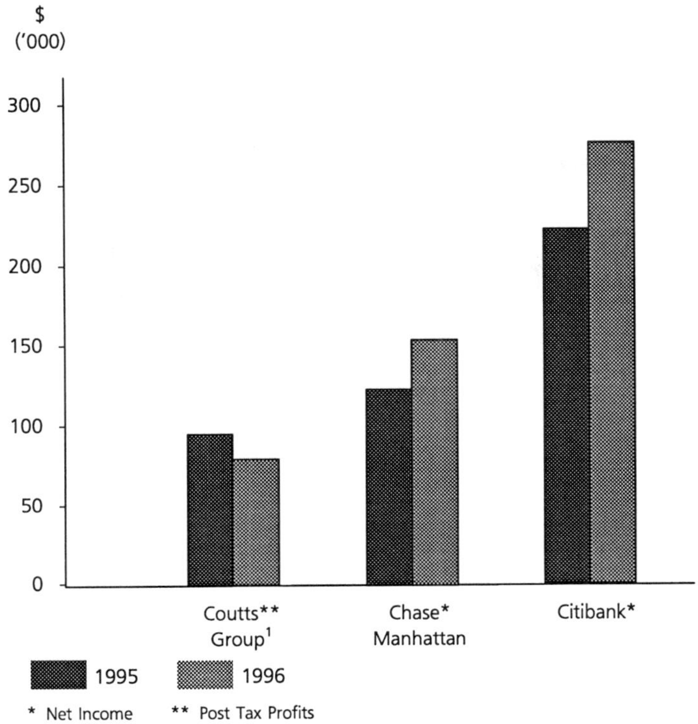

Figure 2.8 Private banking performances 1995/96.

Source: Company Reports.

[1] Converted to US dollars at prevailing rates.

the case of some of the major providers, international private banking is now clearly identified as a core business line.

A survey of providers' business performance inevitably encounters significant differences in the components of private banking activity between one provider and another, and some results include those of domestic private banking. However, the results at least provide a snapshot of comparative scale.

The size of absolute profits made by the Swiss, as with the amount of assets held by them, dwarfs that of other providers. Setting a new precedent, Swiss Bank Corporation reported a net profit in 1996 of $888 million (SFr1.29 billion) and Crédit Suisse, a pre-tax profit of $938 million (SFr1.36 billion).

Notes

1 *World Wealth Report 1997*, Gemini Consulting and Merrill Lynch.

A study, *Economic Freedom of the World 1975–1995*, has created an index to provide an empirical assessment of economic freedom, the central elements being personal choice, protection of private property and freedom of exchange. James Gwartney, Robert Lawson and Walter Block, *Economic Freedom of the World 1975–1995*, pp. 81–88.

2 Lowell L. Bryan, 'The forces transforming global financial markets', *Bank Management*, March/April 1994, pp. 40–45.

Foreign Activity Report, Securities Industry Association, USA.

3 'The rich shall inherit the earth', *The Economist*, 23 November 1996, p. 32; James Gwartney, Robert Lawson and Walter Block, *Economic Freedom of the World 1975–1995*, pp. 81–88.

4 Citicorp 1994 Annual Report.

Crédit Suisse announced on 2 July 1996 a new Crédit Suisse Group with effect from 1997 with four separate business units: domestic banking, private banking, asset management, and corporate/investment banking.

On 21 May 1996 Swiss Bank Corporation set up private banking together with its fund-management arm to form SBC Private Banking with effect from 1997.

Coutts is to be part of National Westminster's new Wealth Management Group with effect from 1 January 1998; the Group also includes Gartmore, NatWest Life and Investment Services and NatWest Ventures.

Union Bank of Switzerland (UBS) is currently under active and vociferous pressure from shareholders, led by Martin Ebner, who claims that the current chief executive has done little to enhance shareholder value. Ebner wants UBS to shed unprofitable businesses, streamline retail banking and abandon proprietary trading and concentrate on asset management. Not alone among Swiss banks, UBS's performance has been lacklustre compared with that of US and European counterparts – UBS produced a 7.5% return in 1995 compared with Barclays' 21%. 'Cuckoo in the nest shatters calm of Swiss Bank industry', *Daily Telegraph*, 13 April 1996; 'Looming shareholder opposition threatens Studer's bid to become Chairman of UBS, *Wall Street Journal Europe*, 16 April 1996, p. 9.

5 *European Private Banking Survey 1996/1997*, Price Waterhouse, p. 39.

6 *World Wealth Report 1997*, Gemini Consulting and Merrill Lynch.

7 Various sources including interviews and *Private Banker International*, June 1996; *South China Morning Post*, 30 September 1995; *Business Times Singapore*, 1 February 1996; *International Private Banking Council Bulletin*, February 1996; Private Banking Survey, *Financial Times*; 19 June 1996; *Executive*, November 1995; *American Banker*, 7 February 1997; Crédit Suisse First Boston Report, January 1997; *The Banker*, January 1997.

8 Arnoldo C. Hax and Nicolas S. Majiluf, *The Strategy Concept and Process, A Pragmatic Approach.*

9 Citicorp 1994 Annual Report and Citicorp 1995 Annual Report; 'More questions, more squirming', *The Economist*, 10 May 1997; 'A question of collaboration', *Financial Times*, 10 and 11 May 1997.

10 Swiss Bank Corporation confirmed that growth of one of its core businesses, private banking, would be through organic growth or acquisition. Chase's portfolio consisted of about $1 billion of assets, with 15 staff responsible for relationships out of New York and Miami. The Standard Chartered sale was part of a number of sales of non-core business lines because its future strategy is to focus on retail and commercial banking and not on being a universal provider. Another sale included Standard Chartered's stockbroking arm, Standard Chartered Securities Ltd. 'Two SBC purchases boost its private client portfolio', *Wall Street Journal Europe*, 24 April 1996, p. 13.

11 *Offshore Finance Yearbook*, 1995.

12 Offshore Red, February 1997, p. 191; 'Taxing Matters', *The Economist*, 5 April 1997; *Global Private Banking*, 20 January 1997, p. 11.

13 *World Wealth Report 1997*, Gemini Consulting and Merrill Lynch, *Price Waterhouse European Private Banking Survey 1996/1997*; *Private Banker International*, March 1997, p. 3; *Private Banker International*, April 1997, p. 7.

Examples of providers that are bearing increased investment costs are Lloyds Private Banking, Coutts and Citibank.

CHAPTER THREE

Asia-Pacific

Introduction

Since the 1980s, the Asia-Pacific region has represented an important new growth area for international private banking services. The region has changed from being one offering predominantly outward referral business to being a regional wealth management opportunity in its own right. Private banking providers have always focused mainly on wealth originating from Hong Kong, which is considered one of the more important markets, also for wealth from other regions that is held there.

With the exception of Singapore, the economic environment in the region is changeable and somewhat uncertain. To a great extent, the cause of the uncertainty is China, increasingly the regional hub. However, in other countries, there is also uncertainty that is the result of local factors.

With strong economic growth across a number of emerging Asian markets, the focus of international private banking has expanded recently to include a number of North East and South East Asian markets - Malaysia, Indonesia, Philippines and Taiwan remain highly regulated but already are targeted for international private banking opportunities.

However, rising above geographic boundaries, the primary target market remains the overseas Chinese who are, by far, the dominant creators and holders of wealth in the region.

Wealth and the wealthy

Of all the regions, it is in Asia where private wealth has grown out of all previously measured historic proportions. It has been estimated that between 1986 and 1996, high net worth individual assets have grow by 337%, a far greater leap than in any other region. This means that the total has risen from $0.8 trillion to $3.5 trillion,[1] accounting for about 20% of total high net worth assets worldwide, behind North America and Europe.

Markets[2]

It is the rapid economic growth in other emerging markets which is the essence of why Asia has become the focus of such close attention by so many international private bankers. In the past Asia was a classic Swiss-based private banking opportunity, principally consisting of wealth that was referred out of the region to Switzerland. However, with the dual forces of economic growth and strong wealth creators in both first and second generations of families, the private banking opportunity has been transformed.

Although recently there has been slow-down in a number of Asian economies, it has been predicted that Asia will account for 50% of the world's GNP by 2020. Underpinning further the diversity of opportunity for private banking services in Asia, it is forecast that Taiwan, Singapore, Hong Kong, South Korea and Malaysia will each grow at nearly twice the rate of any European country in 1997. Certainly, OECD forecasts for 1997–98 give Asian economies the top growth rates among emerging markets.

Nevertheless, the country offering the major market opportunity, despite having one of the smallest populations (6.3 million), has always been Hong Kong, with its high density of wealth. It is perhaps the market in Asia where wealth distribution is most apparent, not just because of family business wealth, but with the emergence of high earning professionals. Three decades of sustained economic growth have made its GDP per capita at $27,130,[4] one of the highest in the world and made Hong Kong the first major private banking market in Asia. Hong Kong is by no means growing at the fastest rate in Asia but with growth in GDP in 1996–97 estimated at between 4% and 5% it is still a favourable rate when compared with those of much of Europe.

As with much wealth in Asia, private wealth creation in Hong Kong is often a family affair and linked tightly with business. Wealth has also been built up through real estate investment and the domestic stock market. Uniquely, much of Hong Kong's offshore market is serviced onshore, thanks to the combination of a benign tax environment, a liberal regulatory environment and the fact that Hong Kong is itself a worldwide financial services centre.

With an expanded market place, the region is now addressed in two halves, with Hong Kong servicing the northern markets and Singapore the southern.

- **Philippines**: During the Marcos years, wealth allegedly flooded out of the country. Economic performance has not been as star-studded as that of other Asian countries. In the 1980s, the economy grew on average less than 2% a year. However, in 1996 GDP grew by 5.5%.

- **Taiwan**: The population is almost exclusively Chinese. As one of the world's top trading nations, Taiwan is expected to show continuing strong economic growth, at around 5% a year. As in other wealth Asian countries, Taiwanese wealthy families tend to invest on a regional basis; they often have significant investment in Hong Kong and also in Mainland China through Hong Kong companies or foreign companies managed in Hong Kong. The fate of Hong Kong and the 'one country–two systems' approach is undoubtedly regarded as a possible precedent for Taiwan. With an uncertain future, political risk is perceived to be high by some wealthy Taiwanese, given the geographic proximity to mainland China and the concentrations of wealth within the region. From an international private banking perspective, Taiwan is one of the more restrictive markets in which to conduct business, in that marketing and advertising of offshore services are not permitted onshore.

In South East Asia, private bankers have more recently been trying to get access to wealth from the following:

- **Singapore**: Its GDP per capita ranks as one of the highest in the world, at $32,878.[4] However, with a population of 3.1 million, the size of the opportunity is relatively small and is typically addressed from outside Singapore.

- **Indonesia**: Wealth is believed to be largely in the hands of overseas Chinese and the Suharto family (known as the 'first family') and its business connections. Economic growth predictions remain good for the short term at around 7%. It remains a strong opportunity for international private bankers despite the somewhat uncertain context - the risk of riots, many racially motivated, and question marks over the future administration, given that President Suharto, now in his seventies, has ruled for 30 years and needs to address the problem of political succession.

- **Thailand**: Old wealth has largely been associated with the Royal Family and the aristocracy. However, new wealth has also been created since mid-1960s as a result of the economic boom, with growth averaging around 7% a year. Economic growth has taken place despite a degree of instability, six coups or attempted coups since 1973, and four elections in the past four years. The opportunity within Thailand has been mixed. It is fairly typical of what is happening in the private banking industry today, in that where domestic stock market performance has been strong, wealthy individuals tend to concentrate, their investments. However, the problems comes when domestic performance tails off, as has happened in the case of the Thai stock market, which fell 30% during 1996.
- **Malaysia**: Among the emerging economies, Malaysia is forecast to have the second-highest economic growth in 1997–98, with GDP growth expected to be about 8%. Wealth is beginning to move away from the Chinese towards the Bumiputras, thanks largely to government policies and actions.

Notwithstanding the diversity of opportunity now presented within Asia-Pacific, Japan and China, are still the economic giants of Asia.

- **Japan**: Economic growth, predicted at 2% in 1997, compares more to those of European industrialised countries than to its Asian counterparts. However, Japan has never really been considered a major international private banking opportunity, given its long-standing exchange control restrictions and the nature of its marketplace, which has comparatively little appetite for international investment.[5] However, given that its wealth has been created largely since the Second World War and that it has high rates of inheritance tax, like other Asian markets it is facing the issue of estate planning and the generational shift of wealth.
- **People's Republic of China (PRC)**: Undoubtedly, high levels of personal wealth are being created today given the

country's status as one of the fastest-growing economies over the last 15 years. Predictions for GDP growth in 1997–98 are the highest of all the emerging economies, averaging around 9–10%, according to the OECD.[6] However, a softly-softly approach has been adopted by most international private banking providers because of the uncertainty of operating guidelines, and most have restricted themselves to the expatriate market so far. The problem of corruption has already been recognised by the PRC authorities and providers alike and is likely to be on-going for the foreseeable future.

- **Australia**: Australia presents limited opportunities compared with other markets in the region, although there are some in connection with first-generation immigrants from Asian countries.
- **India**: With growing deregulation and a relaxing of foreign exchange controls, this market is considered an opportunity both by private bankers and by non-resident Indians who are repatriating wealth to take advantage of domestic opportunities.

Wealth dynamics

Wealth dynamics in Asia are rather one-sided and will continue to be so for some time. What is most evident about Asian wealth is how much of it is owned by overseas Chinese and how they have crossed geographic borders to become one of the richest and most mobile of ethnic groups. It is estimated that there are about 57 million overseas Chinese; 51 million of them in Asia. The largest population of overseas Chinese is in Taiwan but there are also significant populations in Hong Kong, Singapore and Malaysia. According to one estimate, the overseas Chinese in Asia control an economy worth $700 billion and their wealth (cash, gold and shares) may total as much as $2.5 trillion.[3]

It has been estimated that out of the top 1000 companies listed on ten Asian stock markets, overseas Chinese controlled $541 billion of stock or 42% of the total stock. Overseas Chinese own most listed companies in six key Asian countries. In a country-by-country breakdown, their economic power is impressive:[4]

Table 3.1 Population of overseas Chinese and share of economy

	Total (million)	Proportion of population (%)	Wealth as proportion of local economy (%)	GDP contributions (US$ bn)
Hong Kong	6	98	80	120
Singapore	2	76	76	62
Taiwan	21	99	95	255
Malaysia	6	32	60	48
Indonesia	8	4	50	98
Philippines	1	1	40	30
Thailand	6	10	50	80
Vietnam	1	1	20	4
Total	51			697

Source: EIU, Hellmut, Schutte, Insead.

- In Malaysia, 32% of the population are Chinese and they control 62% of the stock market. The seven biggest investors in the Kuala Lumpur Stock Exchange (KLSE) in 1995 were all overseas Chinese; 90% of the smaller and younger companies listed on the KLSE's second exchange are Chinese controlled.
- In the Philippines, the Chinese make up 1% of the population but control over half the stock market.
- In Indonesia, 4% of the population are Chinese yet 75% of the stock market is under their control.
- In Thailand, the Chinese account for at least half the wealth.

In other countries such as Vietnam, Laos, Cambodia and Myanmar, the overseas Chinese economic power is evident. In China itself, overseas Chinese account for about half the foreign direct investment and although their presence is most visible in public listed companies, it is believed that 90% of small and medium-size companies are owned by overseas Chinese.[5]

Super-wealthy families[6]

Increasingly typical of Asia is the extreme wealth of some Asian families. Asia is home to more than one in four of the world's largest fortunes (over $1 billion) with five of the world's ten richest people being Asians. Hong Kong has at least ten families thought to be billionaires. In 1994, there were 46 Asian billionaires, compared with 14 in 1987.

What is remarkable is that the billion-dollar fortunes are self made, from a diverse source of sectors and from a diversity of ethnic origin, not exclusively Chinese. Property development and real estate feature prominently: a common investment and particularly lucrative in Asia. Sources of wealth for the more recent billionaires in Asia are wide ranging and include oil, construction, food, beverages, automobiles, heavy industry, utilities, hotels, pulp and paper, tobacco and beer.

The wealthy

Today, the wealthy in Asia reflect the dominance of entrepreneurs and family businesses together with the emergence of professionals at the lower end of the wealth spectrum. Typically:

- Professionals and senior executives such as doctors, lawyers, bankers, small inheritors and small entrepreneurs, often with investible assets of between US$1 million and US$5 million.
- Business owners who are actively developing their business either as outright owner or part owner, often with investible assets of between US$5 million and US$25 million. This segment tends to have a higher appetite for risk and to use business returns as the performance benchmark for returns on other assets.
- The very wealthy, often entrepreneurs who have sold their business or share of business, and inheritors who are typically members of super-rich families, where investible assets are over US$25 million.

For some private bankers, the expatriate market is considered an opportunity but is principally confined to Japan and Hong Kong.

Attitudes to wealth[7]

The way in which wealthy Asians manage their assets is influenced by a past filled with uncertainty and, in the case of overseas Chinese, by the putting down of new roots out of Mainland China. Research conducted on overseas Chinese entrepreneurs revealed that:

- 90% of the entrepreneurs who were first-generation emigrants had experienced war;
- 40% had been through a political disaster such as the Cultural Revolution;
- 32% had lost a home;
- 28% had weathered economic disasters that resulted in significant loss of wealth.

It is no surprise that many wealthy overseas Chinese have a compartmentalised approach to wealth and control over wealth. Wealth is often split along the following lines:

- Safe-haven money, with monies deposited typically in Switzerland, the Channel Islands and other financial centres in Europe.
- Money to support the extended family who in many cases have migrated to North America, Australia and parts of Europe. There will also have been some planning to cover children's education.
- Internationally diversified wealth, with good investment returns sought abroad, often from real estate in various forms. Real estate has often proven to be lucrative for Chinese investors, particularly in North America, where prices are a fraction of those in Hong Kong, Singapore and Taipei. Investing abroad has the added benefit of political diversification, the cost of which is a slower rate of investment return.
- Wealth that is kept within the region for the wealth holders own business, and for domestic equity investment and domestic real estate.

One of the distinctive characteristics of Asians, whether wealthy or not so wealthy, is the desire for self-management of their investments. Regarding the wealthy, it has been estimated that less than 15% of wealth is made available for professional management. A number of reasons for active self-management can be identified from the strong trading instinct of the Chinese to the fact that alternative indirect investment routes are less developed. Compared with other retail markets worldwide, the unit trust market in Hong Kong has remained relatively small in size and in terms of market penetration. Between 2% and 4% of locals invest by the unit trust route compared with 15% and 20% of investors in Britain and 40% in the USA.

Another important factor is that returns on businesses and real estate investment have been high, reinforcing the belief that Asian investors can do a good job themselves; thereby begging the question of why employ a professional.

Typically, the corporate and personal wealth of a wealthy Asian is hard to separate. A characteristic of many businesses built up in Asia is that wealth can be almost entirely tied up with the business and concentrated within the region. Some of the most common problems concerning wealth that is tied up in business are to do with succession, inheritance and the development of the business. Founding fathers often have difficulty in relinquishing 100% ownership of the business, confusing control of the company with outright ownership.

Needs of the wealthy

Where international private banking services were provided in the past, these were typically provided to overseas Chinese families. The need was almost exclusively for asset protection and a safe haven. Confidentiality and a straightforward discretionary arrangement with a Swiss bank were often the solution.

Today in Asia, the needs of the wealthy differ depending on which slice of wealth in concerned. Wealth that shifts out of the region can be 'rainy day' money and is managed on a different basis, and the traditional discretionary formula of a safe haven still stands today. There has been a shift and a corresponding growth in services, in the following areas:

- **Advisory investment services.** In some ways, the private banking relationship is akin to institutional fund management where a stockbroker advises a fund manager of a particular investment idea. Private bankers typically act as facilitators, feeding investment ideas, and supporting and executing the transaction where a private individual would not be able to do so. Direct investment is common in domestic equities; information and advice is provided across a range of international markets and certain instruments and where the risk profile changes, as for example with structured products, the involvement of the professionals correspondingly increases.
- **Low risk asset growth.** However, not all Asian investors are prepared to invest and trade actively in sophisticated financial instruments. For some markets, where sophistication and the appetite for risk are less, the need is for a more steady

appreciation, and the products selected tend to be more simple offshore deposit and foreign exchange accounts.

- **Corporate product support.** Distinctive in Asia is the level of support private bankers provide to the business activities of their clients. Given that businesses have been one of the major wealth creation vehicles and that personal and business wealth are generally difficult to divide, it is not surprising that private banking providers are sometimes extensively involved in the corporate side of wealth. Corporate services range from those in the area of investment banking such as corporate finance to raise capital and bringing businesses to the market, to corporate banking and trade finance. In the case of businesses which are facing the corporate crossroads, perhaps deciding on international diversification, moving into professional management or outright sale, providers with an investment banking arm can find themselves at a distinct advantage.

In the past, estate planning was not a top priority for Asian family groups. Often succession would have been decided by family members long in advance. There would be strong adherence to the family, and the wishes of the founding father would have been followed to the letter. Low rates of inheritance or estate taxes and in some instances the absence of any form of death duties meant there were no compelling factors to change behaviour and poor regulatory and fiscal enforcement often allowed tax evasion through unsophisticated means.

The environment has now changed and estate planning is of increasing concern to Asian family groups. Although Asia is not a homogeneous planning environment, on the whole it is a low-tax, low-compliance jurisdiction where wealth continues to be generated but where it is common for family members to have migrated and become resident in high-tax, high-compliance jurisdictions.

Furthermore, in many cases, second and third-generation family members are Western educated and tend to have a different view of the importance of estate planning, whereas the patriarch may be more reluctant to address the issue of taxes and generational transfer. Many of these second and third-generation members have emigrated and are now domiciled abroad, for example in the USA. The tax implications of bringing significant non-US assets into the US tax net are very significant when heirs are citizens or 'green card' holders.

The old ways of outright ownership and total control of the business appear incompatible with the reality of the tax bill. If liquidity is an issue, the options revolve around the sale, restructuring and refinancing of the business to guarantee its survival. It can be a difficult bullet to bite but an increasingly important one to address as taxation becomes a major issue. The alternative, when there is a lack of liquidity, is all too evident: the business would have to be sold in order to pay the tax bill.

Part and parcel of estate planning are issues such as:

- Succession and the involvement of the second generation in the business, and cases where the founding father puts pressure on children, perhaps already well established in other careers and professions in North America, Australia or elsewhere, to return to run the family business. The changing social structure of the traditional Chinese family can mean its members are reluctant to do this and, if the business is being restructured, the contract between family management and professional management becomes an issue. The change represents a quantum leap, because in the past businesses have been run by family and kin with little Western formality and structure.
- Business financing and restructuring today often need to be undertaken by professionals whereas traditionally in Chinese families, financing of business has usually been done privately and through the family network.

As far as corporate governance is concerned, although families and individuals dominate as shareholders of listed companies, it is preferred that none of these has dominant control of the company.

Drivers of cross-border wealth

Wealth that has been created in Asia has been created predominantly by overseas Chinese, most of whom left Mainland China after 1949, coming from Shanghai and the coastal provinces such as Guangdon, Fujian and Hainan. Some had education and business know-how, particularly those from Shanghai, and most came with nothing to lose and the desire to achieve security through financial prosperity. Settlement in Asia, particularly in the south-eastern countries such as Malaysia and Indonesia, has not always been smooth, with aggressive anti-Chinese feeling emerging in the 1950s. Shifting of wealth in the early days, therefore, was mainly related to protection of assets, often using Switzerland as the safe haven.

The main factors boosting cross-border wealth are:

- **Diversification of political risk:** A number of uncertainties today relate to China, such as the unresolved future relations between Taiwan and China which came to a head in 1996, now known as the Taiwan missile crisis, when some $200 million allegedly to Labuan;[8] the hand-over of Hong Kong to China in 1997; and the hand-over of Macao to China in 1999.

- **Anonymity:** Secrecy regarding financial affairs remains a strong requirement of many Chinese high net worth individuals. The reasons range from a cultural preference for discretion about their wealth, to alleged aggressive tax avoidance and foreign exchange control infringements.

- **International diversification:** Wealth has tended to flow internationally, following family migration patterns and/or seeking out good investments beyond Asia, where a local network of family, friends and business associates can assist. Notwithstanding this pattern, professionals are needed in order to add value through investment diversification in cases where there is an over-concentration of wealth in Asia because of strong domestic performance and the preference for self-management.

Flight capital from Hong Kong

With the hand-over of Hong Kong to China and the resulting political uncertainty, the issue of flight capital has been raised. Undoubtedly there have been funds flowing out of the region but, on the whole, it is a widely held view within the territory that this is highly characteristic of wealthy Asians. International flows reflect 'business as usual', because better rates of return are always sought beyond the region on the basis that money follows good investment. Evidence of flight capital is often detected in onshore deposits and their sudden removal, as in Latin America. On the contrary, the Hong Kong Monetary Authority reports rising onshore customer deposits between 1993 and 1996.

Confirming the sound opportunity that Hong Kong presents to the Asian investor, since the Joint Declaration was signed in 1984 and up until the period just before the hand-over, the picture has been one of positive economic performance, with GDP per capita increasing by 400%, the Hang Seng Index up by more than 100%, stock market capitalisation up by 1200% and stock market turnover up by 4700%.

Asian financial centres[9]

Financial centres within Asia are generally either giants or dwarfs. The major centres are Hong Kong, Singapore and Tokyo. Tokyo, because of regulations, has no offshore business to speak of, whereas Singapore and Hong Kong are the leading financial centres for private wealth management.

Hong Kong

Hong Kong has taken over from Shanghai as the commercial centre of Asia and is both its commercial and financial centre. It is ranked as one of the leading offshore centres worldwide, attracting about 5–10% of the world's offshore private wealth. Its attractions for north Asian markets such as the Philippines, South Korea and Taiwan are its reputation for banking secrecy and its well-regulated financial infrastructure.

Hong Kong is also the fund-management centre of Asia, helped by the liberal tax regime for fund managers. Although business costs such as salaries are high, overall business efficiency too is high. Some fund management has been attracted to Singapore and Malaysia for their business development opportunities and, to some degree, because they represent a safety net.

Uncertainty of future has been a characteristic of Hong Kong for much of its history. On the other hand, since the transition period began in 1985, after the signing of the Joint Declaration, reciprocal investment between China and Hong Kong has been extensive, with Hong Kong benefiting from the opening up of a huge new market.

Since the mid 1980s, many companies have shifted domicile and it has been estimated that 86% of local businesses incorporated over the last six years are technically domiciled elsewhere. Whether international groups today would use Hong Kong companies to consolidate their regional business interests as they once did is somewhat uncertain. However, the decision to go elsewhere can be motivated as much by the cost of operating out of Hong Kong as by the political environment.

On 1 July 1997, China resumed sovereignty over Hong Kong, which is now a Special Administrative Region of the People's Republic of China. The Joint Declaration, signed by Margaret Thatcher and Zhao Zi Yang in 1984, spells out how Hong Kong's economic status will remain unchanged for 50 years after the transition, particularly how its status as an international financial centre is to be maintained. The Joint Declaration and Basic Law includes China's agreement to the retention of Hong Kong's monetary, legal, financial and tax systems. This means the continuance of a low-tax policy, no foreign exchange controls, the convertibility of the Hong Kong dollar and the peg with the US dollar.

Although Shanghai is regaining its status as a major business centre, it is unlikely that it will eclipse Hong Kong as an international centre. More than likely, it will remain focused on the domestic market and a situation will emerge similar to that of the USA where a number of financial centres exist, each with different focus - New York, Chicago and Los Angeles.

Singapore

Singapore's principal source of wealth is its financial sector, and given its size of economy and population, it has a disproportionate number of financial institutions. It is currently the fourth-largest centre for foreign exchange trading, with over 200 commercial and merchant banks and 100 fund management companies.

With its geographic position in South East Asia, it is a staging post for marketing private banking services to other South East Asian countries such as Malaysia, Thailand and Indonesia.

In Singapore, there are no foreign exchange restrictions and no capital gains tax. However, income from interest and dividends are taxable. It is highly regulated with a clean reputation. The lack of corruption makes Singapore (and Hong Kong for that matter) stand apart from other Asian countries.

Singapore and Hong Kong are often contrasted as financial centres and distinctions are made between the liberal evolution in Hong Kong and the prescriptive style of government in Singapore.

Labuan

Malaysia is aiming to establish Labuan, located off the coast of Borneo, as a competitive response to other leading offshore centres. In 1996 Labuan had 52 licensed offshore banks in operation, of which 45 were foreign owned. The Malaysian government is hoping that out of small acorns grow great trees; 700,000 offshore companies are registered so far. However, Labuan appears to be setting high standards when issuing banking licences, and making clear that only the larger institutions are desirable.

Labuan's main disadvantage is that it is a late entrant to an overcrowded sector in which Singapore and Hong Kong are the established private banking centres. Also, some private bankers will attest to perceived nervousness on the part of some clients about the robustness of Labuan's banking confidentiality. Perhaps it is more a question of being too close to home for some. However, Labuan's prime advantage is that it is a zero-tax haven, unlike Singapore and Hong Kong.

In addition, it has aspirations to develop as the leading offshore centre for Islamic wealth, complementing the growing Islamic banking market within Malaysia.

Other smaller financial centres

There are a number of small islands with banking sectors within the Asia-Pacific region. The Marshall Islands, Cook Islands, Vanuatu and Western Samoa all participate in international private banking and allow for real-time business to be conducted, given the time zones they are in.

Non-Asian financial centres

Wealth destinations outside Asia are in the Americas and Europe, and selection generally follows family migration patterns, except for Switzerland. The other major wealth centres for Asian wealth are:

- London for its wide international investment infrastructure;
- Channel Islands for estate-planning purposes;
- Switzerland for confidentiality and asset protection;
- Bermuda where large numbers of previously incorporated businesses in Hong Kong have now been domiciled, including Jardine Matheson;
- Luxembourg where no taxes for non-residents and no withholding tax or tax on capital gains make it an attractive destination for wealth originating from Asia.

Table 3.2 Notable international private banking providers in Asia

US banks	Chase Manhattan, Citibank, Merrill Lynch
US investment banks	JP Morgan, Goldman Sachs
Swiss commercial banks	Crédit Suisse, Union Bank of Switzerland, Swiss Bank Corporation
Smaller Swiss banks	Lombard Odier, Pictet
European commercial banks	Coutts, ABN Amro, Rabobank, Dresdner Bank, Commerzbank, HSBC, Banque Nationale de Paris, Banque Indosuez, Crédit Lyonnais, Banque Paribas
Offshore specialists	Bank of Bermuda, Butterfield Trust (Hong Kong); lawyers

Competition[10]

The internationally wealthy in Asia are served by foreign institutions and a number of relationships usually exist. The present of private banking providers has changed dramatically over the last decade. International private banking began in the time-honoured way of asset gathering with assets typically going to Switzerland for safe keeping because there was no servicing support within the region. Then, foreign banks operating within the region, such as Standard Chartered and Hongkong Bank, with the headstart of their consumer franchise, began to focus on their more wealthy customers, and were shortly followed by Citibank.

While the traditional private banking providers have been heading to Asia in huge numbers, so have the non-traditional providers which have diversified into servicing the wealthy. Even today, despite the large number of providers some well established, new entrants are still arriving in Hong Kong and Singapore, suggesting that the region is fast approaching saturation, particularly in Hong Kong, where differentiation is hard to find.

Additionally, typical of Asia, are providers of corporate services that involve the setting up and administering of offshore companies. This is big business in Asia and can be highly profitable for providers of these services such as lawyers; moreover they can offer competitive prices compared with large, all-service providers.

Competitive activity reflects the importance of Asia as a private banking region, the shifting political spectrum – particularly the handover of Hong Kong to China, and the need for greater representation throughout the region in order to have access new markets. Those providers that can also offer services in support of family emigration patterns to Australia, Canada and North America as well as being able to support local investment opportunities have a significant competitive strength.

Asia is now seen as an important profit centre by a number of international providers. The key areas identified for corporate growth are investment banking and private banking, and the opportunities are deemed such that the dominant Swiss providers are openly and increasingly committing themselves to Asia, in a way not seen in other regions. Union Bank of Switzerland is expanding in South East Asia with a view to private banking (and Asia) being a growing contributor to its worldwide profits.

Expansion generally has consisted largely in establishing a private banking position in Singapore. Reasons for establishing a position in Singapore have been twofold; firstly, to provide clients with a choice of offshore centre, if Hong Kong proves less attractive than it once did; secondly, to be geographically nearer the emerging markets in South East Asia such as Malaysia, Thailand and Indonesia.

There has been extensive reorganisation of providers at international level, with many of the major providers establishing clearer operating lines, additional headquarters and stronger focus on new markets.

If pessimism exists regarding Hong Kong and its future as an international private banking centre, this is not reflected in the recruitment activity. Recruitment is on the increase both in Hong Kong and Singapore with staff numbers almost doubling in some instances. However, given that many key providers are engaged in recruitment drives and expansion, it is unclear where the skilled individuals are genuinely coming from.

The ability to provide confidentiality and an international presence is as important a criterion in provider selection as personal rapport with the private banker and performance. Furthermore, cultural affinities coupled with product innovation are the keys which explain why the private banking scene is dominated by Citibank and some of the European providers with historical links with the region, such as HSBC.

Strategies[11]

The focus is not only on geography but also on wealth levels. The very top end of the market is considered to be where investible assets reach $50 million and key providers include JP Morgan and Goldman Sachs. Most providers focus on investible assets above $1 million; but that would very much be the minimum level.

Growth

It is a firmly held view in the private banking industry that private banking is a referral business and there are no quick routes to market share. Apart from cases where private banking business has been an integral part of a group acquisition, there has been a veritable absence of stand-alone private banking acquisitions. However, in 1996, Swiss Bank Corporation bought a major market share of Asian wealth by acquiring the international private banking book of Standard Chartered, believed to have some $5 billion under management for about 4000 individuals in the Asia-Pacific region at a cost of between 1% and 3% of assets under management. Standard Chartered, even though estimated to be one of the larger private banking players in Asia, had decided to focus exclusively on core businesses.

Generally though, growth is through referrals. Few providers anywhere in the private banking business in the world have such a deeply embedded franchise in one of the wealthiest markets as HSBC Private Banking, one of the leading private banking providers in Asia. With a pan-Asian franchise and 215 retail branches in Hong Kong alone and a full range of commercial and investment banking services, it is the only international private banking provider in Asia with such a foothold, now that Standard Chartered has withdrawn.

It seems that the engine for growth is the hiring of people and certainly in Hong Kong and Singapore there have been spurts of recruitment. There is noticeable investment in marketing and relationship managers on the ground, particularly focusing on the newer markets. While providers are indeed increasing their staff numbers, there are huge differences in scale compared with the larger providers; Citibank for example is estimated to have about 200 relationship managers focusing on private banking in Asia (excluding Japan) and HSBC Private Banking about 100.

Delivery and distribution

For such a discreet business, private banking is conversely highly visible in the employment market. It is more characteristic of Asia than any of other region for key managers (and their teams) to up sticks and move from one house to another. What this highlights is a skill shortage and a seller's market and private banking providers are paying increasingly high premiums for staff. It has also come to the notice of some of the authorities, who obviously consider this to be unnecessary destabilising force. In Singapore in particular the

Association of Banks has issued a warning to providers who contribute to the problem of staff-poaching.

Local regulations as well as customers dictate the need for tailored delivery and distribution strategies in Asia. A presence in Hong Kong and Singapore is considered the minimum requirement for an international private banking provider. Expansion beyond these two locations generally has been in the form of representative offices or offshore banking units, given local restrictions. Gaining access to local markets can be difficult, with quotas imposed on the number of foreign banks operating, together with restrictions on the marketing of offshore services. Some of the larger providers have representative offices in Jakarta, Bangkok, Taipei and Manila.

Products and services

The provider's product portfolio is perhaps more important to an Asian client than to other private banking clients worldwide. Although the relationship manage is still of key importance, it is the products and the specifically tailored product options that can clinch and maintain the relationship. It is by no means universal that providers offer all of the core products and services. Typically, the advisory and investment services are central with only the bigger and the more specialised providers being able to seamlessly provide and co-ordinate corporate and investment services.

Core products and services are:

- **Advisory services** including equities in the home market, foreign exchange and options trading, and structured products using a range of currencies and indices. Lending too is very important for leveraging the investment potential with back-to-back arrangements being typical. Given some of the more speculative trading, lending arrangements are often done only on a secured basis.
- **Investment services** including discretionary fund management and investment funds.
- **Trusts**, particularly offshore trusts, are increasingly used by wealthy Asians as a means of dealing with inheritance tax and estate duties. Those from Hong Kong were probably the first of the wealthy Asian families to start using trusts, beginning in the early 1980s when significant emigration began. To support emigration and in recognition of the move to a higher tax

environment, the pre-emigration trust, the foreign grantor trust for the US and the Canadian 60-month shelter trust became widely used. Greater cross-border investment has also provided an incentive for the use of sophisticated offshore trusts. Trusts have cultural appeal as they can provide anonymity rather than just a will which anyone has the right to inspect after the death of an individual. Trusts are also used for income tax planning; holding assets through foreign companies has made it possible in some circumstances to avoid capital gains and income tax charges, in cases where a country levies these on a worldwide basis for its residents.

- **Corporate and investment banking services** ranging from trade finance and bills of exchange to equity raising, flotation and sales of businesses.

Other services include:

- Personal banking services which can be supported worldwide only by the larger providers such as Citibank, Chase Manhattan Bank and HSBC Private Banking with their group resources.
- The purchase of art, jewellery and antiques, which is becoming increasingly common among Asians, although not usually through private banking providers.

Regulatory and legislative environment

At both corporate and personal level, a number of moves have been made by the Revenue authorities to deal with tax avoidance, closing in on loopholes and making certain activities potentially criminal. In general, the growing trend among the authorities in Asia is towards greater enforcement. This has meant introducing legislation to ensure that the authorities have the teeth to address what is deemed as aggressive tax avoidance, verging on tax evasion. An example of this is in Indonesia, where the tax system is under review and certain changes are already evident. Some basic 'controlled companies' provisions were passed into law in 1994, making it a legal requirement for an Indonesian resident tax payer who is the controlling stockholder to declare income and gains within six months of the end of the tax year, if not, this will be deemed as tax fraud.

Estate planning – estate duties and inheritance tax

High rates of estate duties and inheritance tax provide opportunities for estate planning services for international private bankers.

- In Japan, rates of inheritance tax and gift tax are at 70%; the generation with the wealth is not the generation with the problem.
- The Philippines has inheritance and gift taxes; the former is levied at 35%, and was recently halved from 70% to encourage payment. It is a civil law jurisdiction and has no trust concept in its jurisprudence. Statutory heirship exists.
- In Taiwan, estate tax and gift tax are high with marginal rates levied at 60% on worldwide assets of a Taiwanese domiciled individual and on the Taiwanese-sited assets of a non-domiciliary individual.
- In Indonesia, there are no inheritance, estate or gift taxes. It is a civil law jurisdiction that derives most of its jurisprudence from the Dutch, combined with elements of *Shari'a*.

Exchange controls

These still exist across a number of countries, varying in the level of restriction and the compliance requirements:

- Japan has recently raised the amount allowed to be taken out of the country to US$900 000.
- The Philippines in 1994 abolished exchange controls that had prevented Philippine nationals from freely converting pesos into foreign currency, although some form of monitoring of the purchase of pesos by foreign investors still exists.
- In Malaysia, official notification to the central bank is required for any movement of capital over US$40 000.

Conclusions and outlook

High net worth individual assets in Asia have grown 337% in 1986–96, by far the greatest leap of any other region, to $3.5 trillion.[1] It has been predicted that Asia will overtake North America to become the second largest wealth pool behind Europe by the turn of the century.

Hong Kong remains one of the most important markets, although beginning to mature, compared with the newly emerging markets particularly in South East Asia, where economic growth is predicted to be some of the highest of all emerging markets worldwide. Thailand, Philippines, Malaysia, Indonesia are still key markets. China with a huge latent potential has yet to be addressed in any substantial way and nor will it be in the immediate future.

Asia is still characterised by uncertainty and by the traditional drivers of cross-border wealth. Wealth flows are typically from the less regulated and less onerous tax environment of Asia to more highly regulated and more highly taxed environments of North America, parts of Europe and Australia, following family migration patterns or going where it makes sense to invest.

Asia is also home to the super-wealthy, and increasingly so. These families are not exclusively Chinese, but the overseas Chinese are nevertheless the single largest holders of wealth, almost to the exclusion of other ethnic origins. Their economic power is most evident in Hong Kong, Malaysia, Philippines, Indonesia and Thailand.

Except in Malaysia, there is not a significant shift of wealth away from the overseas Chinese population. Wealth is largely linked to family businesses although in Hong Kong in particular, the emerging wealthy are becoming more evident, specifically the high-earning professionals and the smaller inheritors.

Asia represents a unique private banking proposition compared with other regions. At the heart of its service is a highly tuned advisory service supporting wealthy individuals in their trading activity and their appetite for actively pursuing capital growth across a range of risk-graded products. Asian private banking is beginning to rival the Swiss style of private banking as a distinctive proposition for the wealthy that combines active management with high levels of technological support and personal attention.

The product portfolio is perhaps more important to an Asian client than to most other private banking clients worldwide. Core products and services are advisory services, investments, and corporate and investment banking services, with trusts being increasingly important. Typically a wealthy Asian manages and trades in domestic equities and needs professional support where international equities are traded or where the risk profile increases as in the case of derivatives, and where direct access is not possible.

One difference between product providers is in the area of corporate support and it concerns how far the support is integrated with the traditional services tailored to the personal wealth. One of the largely unmet needs is the tax-efficient transfer of generational wealth, which is forcing the founding fathers to look at tax, succession and the problem of children unwilling to take over the business.

Hong Kong, the long-established centre for private banking services, is now being challenged by Singapore, which is growing in importance in the region. Singapore is largely an offshore servicing centre for the South East Asian markets but, where the larger providers are concerned, it can be comforting for clients to know that there is an alternative to Hong Kong in the event of fears growing over China's future policies. Labuan is not considered a threat at this stage to either Hong Kong or Singapore.

Like Europe, the region is over-banked, particularly in Hong Kong and this is likely to get worse with the growing presence of providers in Singapore. HSBC Private Banking and Citibank have the major advantages of strong branding, scale and an extensive group franchise to farm. However, acquisition has strengthened Swiss Bank Corporation's foothold in the region. Generally, though, growth is achieved through referrals.

International private banking is highly visible in the employment market, reinforcing the perception that there is a skill shortage in all levels of private banking in Asia.

There has been little expansion of private banking offices beyond Hong Kong and Singapore. With uncertainty in the region, onshore servicing has yet to be developed to any significant extent and it is not considered a particularly important client requirement.

Aggressive tax avoidance is coming under pressure with moves across the region to start addressing loopholes and non-tax payment. This bodes well for those providers who have the technical trust and tax back-up to provide tax planning solutions for wealthy Asians who send their funds to more highly regulated and highly taxed jurisdictions.

Notes

1 *World Wealth Report 1997*, Gemini Consulting and Merrill Lynch.

2 'What drives Deutsche Bank in Asia', *Financial Times*, 13 November 1997; GDP figures are extracted from *The World in 1997*, Economist Intelligence Unit. Although a number of markets worldwide are showing a growing share of equity investment, this is not the case in Japan where there appears to be a continuous reduction in stock market investments' share of financial assets, with equity commitment

less than one-third of that in the USA. Bumiputras make up approximately 54% of Malaysia's population. A Bumiputra is defined in the Constitution as one who practises Islam, speaks Bahasa and follows Malay custom in the home.

3 'Survey: Business in Asia', *The Economist*, 9 March 1996.

4 'Survey: Business in Asia', *The Economist*, 9 March 1996.

5 John Naisbitt, *Megatrends Asia*, p. 4.

6 'The Superrich', *Forbes*, 15 July 1996, pp. 124–127; 'Trillionaire Club', *Asia Inc.*, November 1994, p. 32.

7 'Overseas Chinese hungry for LA property', *Sunday Morning Post*, 23 February 1997, p. 5; 'Chase to build advisory units worldwide', *Global Private Banker*, 19 February 1996, p. 16; 'Old habits die hard as cagey HK investors play own hands', *Sunday Morning Post*, 23 February 1997. The Worldwide web of Chinese Business, The Evolving Global Economy, edited by Kenichi Ohmae, Harvard Business Review (1995).

8 *Asia Inc.*, July 1996, p. 29.

9 Crédit Suisse First Boston, January 1997; 'Territory force to be reckoned with in Asia', *Sunday Morning Post*, 23 February 1997; 'Banker's worry about Hong Kong's future', *American Banker*, 1 July 1996; 'Social price to be paid for rewards from China future', *South China Morning Post*, 16 September 1996; 'Nation's banking industry exerts disproportionate global influence for its small size', *Financial Times*, 8 February 1996; 'Singapore', *Global Private Banking*, 11 December 1995, p. 10; 'Making Labuan an Islamic IOFC', *New Straits Times*, 24 January 1997.

10 Union Bank of Switzerland 1995 Annual Report; 'Bruising battle for Asian dominance', *Euromoney*, August 1996, p. 90; 'UBS seeks investment banking Asian growth', Reuters News Service, 17 August 1995; *European Private Banking Survey, 1996/1997*, Price Waterhouse; 'Crédit Suisse has made Singapore its regional headquarters'; 'Banque Nationale de Paris has created a new private banking entity called BNP Private Bank Asia'; 'Demand for private banking services increased due to apprehensions regarding the country's turnover to China in 1997', *Asian Wall Street Journal*, 31 October 1995, p. 20.

11 'Two SBC Purchases Boost Its Private Client Portfolio', *Wall Street Journal Europe*, 24 April 1996, p. 13. It is estimated that Citibank has 200 private banking representatives in Asia (excluding Japan) compared with Deutsche Bank and Banque Indosuez which reportedly have about 50 each; 'Singapore: Association warns against banks against poaching staff', *Business Times* (Singapore), 5 July 1995; 'What do you buy after you've got the private plane?' *Forbes*, 12 February 1996, p. 106.

CHAPTER FOUR
Europe

Introduction

Europe is the headquarters of international private banking. The strength of Europe, as a geographical region, derives from a number of factors. It is the worldwide centre for fund administration, a position that is continually strengthened by developments in Dublin and Luxembourg. When compared with other regions, Europe is unique for the wide spectrum of wealth it attracts from around the globe, making London, Switzerland and the Channel Islands the largest centres for private banking wealth. But it is Switzerland that has always led the way in the industry. Switzerland, in the company of Austria, Luxembourg and Liechtenstein, has long been a siren to the wealthy who want banking confidentiality and cast-iron protection of their wealth.

As the funds flow indicates, Europe is undoubtedly considered one of the more attractive regions for wealth management from a client's perspective. From the provider's perspective, though, Europe has one of the most competitive operating environments. Even the firmly established providers, like the Swiss, have been forced to change their ways and compete more actively for a share of cross-border wealth.

In a worldwide context, Europe has a significant proportion of old wealth. To a great extent, international private banking providers are rebalancing their efforts and geographic focus more towards other regions where the new wealth appears more accessible than in Europe. Spurring them on is Europe's economic performance, which recently has been relatively lacklustre compared with that of some of the Asian economies, for example. At home in Europe, the marketplace has expanded through the opening up of the previously communist-ruled Eastern and Central European countries. However, as in any emerging market, while there are undoubtedly growing levels of private wealth, the opportunity is somewhat unpredictable, and not considered universally attractive by private banking providers.

Wealth and the wealthy

Europe is now estimated to be the world's largest wealth pool of high net worth assets, overtaking North America which dominated in the 1980s. Between 1986 and 1996, European high net worth assets grew from $2 trillion to $5 trillion. Further estimates predict Europe's continuing dominance up to the year 2000. However, unlike the USA and Asia, wealth in Europe has traditionally been associated with inheritance, old wealth and more traditional forms of asset growth rather than entrepreneurial wealth creation.

Markets

In line with other regions, the opportunities in Europe for international private banking providers rest on a number of distinctive factors. Wealth once driven across borders by instability remains a large and important opportunity today, as inheritance and a change of beneficial owner can often mean a change in relationship and different client demands. Wealth protection is another market requirement, given that Europe generally can be characterised as a high-tax jurisdiction. With lacklustre economic performance in the recent past, the provision of international investment management reflects a worldwide trend to properly diversified portfolios of assets.

- **North European markets such as UK, France and Germany:** These markets are some of the more competitive, given their highly developed financial services infrastructure and capital markets. Many of the opportunities are largely tax-driven in nature.
- **Italy:** Political instability, lack of domestic competition and lack of possibilities for domestic investment have made Italy a

classic international private banking opportunity. Typically wealth flows to Switzerland, because of its proximity.

- **Spain and Portugal:** Significant amounts of old wealth have been held outside these markets because of their past political profile.
- **Benelux countries:** These markets are often addressed as a tightly knit group of market opportunities with domestic providers expanding across borders, where funds flow, often for tax reasons.
- **Eastern and Central European countries:** In **Russia,** wealth is sourced primarily from the formation of new businesses and the privatisation of firms. However, it is an uncertain market opportunity with political instability, crime and corruption and the lack of a secure legal framework in which private bankers can operate. Economic progress is found in particular in the **Czech Republic**, the richest of the former communist countries and **Poland**, where growth rates are about 6% and where small businesses are forming at a much faster rate than in Russia.
- **Scandinavia and Germany** represent niche markets where wealth is tied up in privately owned companies. In Germany, it is estimated that within the Mittelstand, there is a significant amount of privately held wealth which could be released over the next five years as a result of succession, which will affect 250 000 companies. **Greece** is also identified as a market for new wealth.

Other opportunities relate to the changing regulatory and legislative environments at both domestic and regional level:

- **Threatened or suddenly imposed changes in taxes:** One of the recent changes in taxation in Germany has created an on-going controversy relating to supposed tax evasion.
- **European Union markets:** Particularly in relation to the marketing and distribution of investment funds.

Drivers moving wealth offshore within Europe

Europe has been a classic international private banking market where two world wars and the existence of extreme forms of government have driven wealth 'cross border'. These conditions mainly affected old wealth and the older generation, and private bankers detect a shift towards legitimate tax avoidance and international investment as the new generation takes over from the old. Helping this along is the changed interest-rate environment which in some markets is encouraging investors to turn more to equities and less to local currency. However, the older generation of wealthy individuals still maintain money outside their country of origin because for some, old habits die hard. Safety and wealth protection are still perceived to be significant factors.

European financial centres

Europe manages the largest share of cross-border wealth, defined as wealth held outside its country of origin. It has been estimated that approximately 60–80% of the world's cross-border wealth is managed within Europe, with some 35–45%, or approximately \$1.8 trillion, in Switzerland.[2] Whereas Switzerland was once the only choice, for a private banking client seeking to place monies outside their country of residence, Europe now offers an extensive range of centres including a number of tax havens.

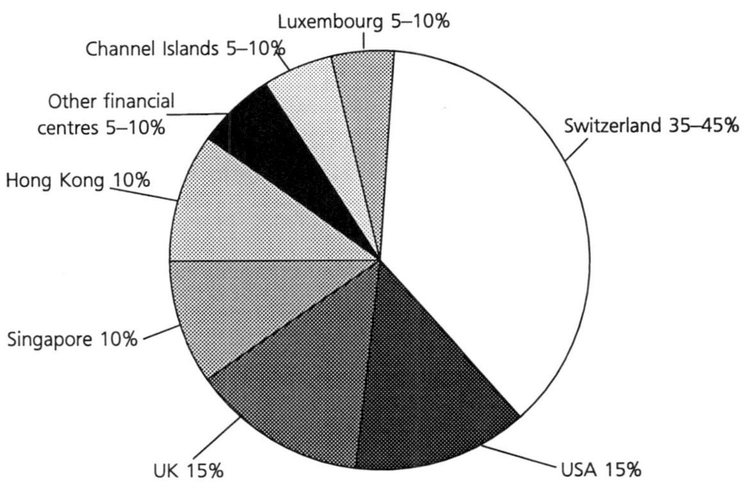

Figure 4.1 World's cross-border wealth destined for Europe.
Source: Crédit Suisse First Boston, January 1996.

Switzerland

With few natural resources of its own, Switzerland has concentrated heavily on promoting itself as an international onshore financial centre. Until the 1960s it was the principal centre for cross-border wealth; a safe haven, rather than a tax haven, for money deposited and allegedly where providers asked few questions about the wealth left there. Its attributes for international private banking are its predictable and stable financial and political environment; long-standing expertise in multi-currency investment; its banking secrecy laws; its geographic location which enables it to be a servicing centre for international clients; and its cultural diversity and multilingual nature.

Rather than a single centre, it is in fact four - Geneva, Zürich, Lugano and Basle - each with a distinct history and operating environment to attract wealth from different non-European and European sources. Linguistic affinity and geographic proximity influence the direction in which funds flow within Europe, particularly for French, Italian and German speakers. However, the two main centres are in Geneva and Zürich, which have always competed with one another to be the international private banking centre of the world. Geneva probably does better than Zürich in attracting clients from certain areas of the world such as the Middle East, Latin America and France.

The problems concerning Switzerland are those relating to cost, namely its high operational costs, stamp duty and its 35% withholding tax (one of the highest in the world), and its banking secrecy law. The pressure being brought to bear from the international community continues to highlight the differences in Swiss banking regulations.[6]

As Switzerland is not a member of the European Union (EU), there are some areas of uncertainty as to how its standing as a financial centre for private banking wealth may be affected. What should not be underestimated is the longevity and durability of Switzerland's position in international private banking, despite the levelling-out of competition between centres.

London[3]

London, like New York, is a worldwide centre for all global financial services. It is attractive to international private banking clients with its leading position in international equities, foreign exchange, bonds and derivatives. With the help of London's highly developed capital markets infrastructure, money managers in the City have built themselves a reputation for an aggressive and sophisticated investment house-style. Although London was a comparative backwater for international private banking until the 1980s, the view is often expressed that it is now eclipsing Switzerland in attracting new cross-border wealth that is looking for strong investment performance. This may well be true, but the size of funds managed overall within Switzerland continues to dwarf that of funds managed in London.

From a provider's perspective, the UK has a stringent operating environment that has significantly contributed to the raising of standards including, not least, the requirement for professional qualifications. It is unlikely that either the scope of the regulations or the cost of compliance will lessen significantly.

Like Switzerland, the UK is a key servicing centre for international clients; it is also, like Luxembourg, a member of the EU. There is a general sense of optimism with regard to the consequences of European Monetary Union (EMU) and the future position of London, whether or not the UK signs up to EMU.

Luxembourg

Luxembourg is more a financial centre for investment funds than a tax haven and for this reason is less of a private banking centre *per se* and more a European financial centre. Its private banking clients are mostly individuals and single-purpose companies, referrals from neighbouring countries, or they are nationals resident abroad. However, it does have characteristics which place it on a competitive footing with Switzerland for international private banking funds, particularly those from Germany, France and Belgium that are looking for a less discriminating tax environment in Luxembourg.

For the future, Luxembourg is facing a number of issues, particularly as a member of the EU. Its banking secrecy rules (established under criminal law) are more stringent than those in other EU members. However, this secrecy will continue to be subject to the continuing harmonisation of EU laws and regulations, particularly with regard to withholding tax, for which currently Germany is calling for uniformity. Luxembourg will accept such a tax only if all OECD countries conform (and this would include Switzerland). Harmonisation within the EU would benefit Switzerland and the Channel Islands.

Corporate tax is one of the highest in Europe (40%) and puts Luxembourg at a disadvantage compared with London and Dublin, where the taxes are about 30% and 10% respectively. Personnel costs, although not as high as Switzerland, are also a problem.

Channel Islands

The Channel Islands started to emerge as competition to Switzerland in the 1960s and are renowned worldwide for their product specialisation, particularly in trusts and corporate structures, which actively compete with the anonymity provided through Swiss services. As a consequence, the Channel Islands are attracting increasing levels of cross-border wealth and are expected to grow from strength to strength. Although they are Crown Dependencies of the UK, they are not part of the EU and are therefore not bound by EU banking restrictions and tax laws. Together with London, they are considered the main competition to Switzerland for cross-border wealth.

- **Jersey:** As an international financial centre and tax haven, Jersey has some of the largest and most reputable institutions, offering retail and corporate services. However, for the international private banking industry, its main attractions are its product specialisation, its banking secrecy and its position as a tax haven.

- **Guernsey:** Guernsey maintains its distinction from Jersey and other European centres through its specialisation as a leading centre for captive insurance companies. It also offers a developed administered banking facility. However, as an international private banking centre, it has similar characteristics to Jersey, being a tax haven which levies non-residents with income tax only on income arising in Guernsey; there is no taxation on capital gains and no withholding tax.

Other European centres

Other significant centres in Europe are Dublin and Liechtenstein.

- **Dublin** is seen as one of the more attractive international private banking centres of the future and indeed, it has been dubbed as 'Europe's back-office'. With corporation tax at 10%, Dublin is strongly positioned to attract investment funds, particularly UCITS (Undertaking for Collective Investment in Transferable Securities). Writers, artists and composers can live in Ireland free of tax on any artistic earnings.

- **Liechtenstein's** attractions reside in its political and economic stability. In addition, it offers low levels of taxation, no assistance to foreign judiciaries in connection with tax matters, no withholding tax and stringent banking legislation. Special features of Liechtenstein are its trusts (being the only European continental country to have trust regulations), notably its Gesellschaftswesen for the company sector; foundations such as Stiftungen (which is similar to English and American trusts); and the Anstalt, long-established international private banking products, particularly for tax and estate planning.

Other smaller centres include the following:

- The **Isle of Man**, a Crown Dependency, has been steadily rebuilding its reputation as a financial centre since the collapse in 1982 of the Savings and Investment Bank that hit the island severely.
- **Austria**, although politically and economically stable, has a relatively weak banking sector. However, it is renowned for its strict banking secrecy laws.
- **Monaco** attracts monies from Italy. It is a tax haven with no tax on private income and no restrictions on foreigners owning property.
- **Malta** attracts Middle Eastern money and competes with Bahrain.
- **Madeira** appeals to expatriates of European Portuguese origin and to Latin American countries which have strong Portuguese communities.
- **Cyprus**, because of its geographic position, attracts funds in particular from the Middle East and from the former Soviet Union.
- **Gibraltar** is a small international centre and continues to be affected by the uncertainty created by the dispute between the UK and Spain about sovereignty over the territory.

Notwithstanding the range of choice and the developments within centres, the major centres remain Switzerland, London, the Channel Islands and Luxembourg. It is widely believed that although difficult to estimate, most European wealth does stay within the geographic borders of Europe. However, it seems certain that a small percentage goes to New York and the Cayman Islands, which can provide 'Anglo-Saxon' trusts, and some high net worth individuals from the Netherlands use the Dutch Antilles.

Table 4.1 Notable international private banking

Privately owned banks	16 Swiss private banks
Swiss commercial banks	Crédit Suisse, Swiss Bank Corporation, Union Bank of Switzerland
European commercial	Coutts, Lloyds Bank, HSBC, Dresdner Bank, Deutsche Bank, Barclays Bank, ABN Amro
US banks	Citibank, Chase Manhattan Bank
US investment banks	JP Morgan, Goldman Sachs, Merrill Lynch, Morgan Stanley
Family controlled banks	Rothschild; Safra Republic, Bank J Vontobel, Bank Julius Baer
Asset managers	Global Asset Management and asset management arms of European banks
Boutiques	Soros

Competitive environment[4]

International private banking in Europe has been part and parcel of a rapid evolution of financial liberalisation during the last two decades which has resulted in a highly diverse financial services sector. Overall, new financial institutional types have emerged, producing a vastly different competitor profile in Europe. Today, the scene is heavily peppered with sizeable and worldwide bank providers, regional and niche bank providers, and a strong presence of non-bank providers.

However, notwithstanding the overall size of wealth managed within Europe, apart from Crédit Suisse, Swiss Bank Corporation and Union Bank of Switzerland, which between them reputedly manage about half of Switzerland's cross-border wealth an estimated $0.9 trillion,[2] no other provider has a very large share of the business yet, even though in some cases the shares might be growing fast. Overall, the management of cross-border wealth in Europe is highly fragmented.

Indigenous European institutions dominate the region's international private banking activities. Non-European providers, although increasingly successful, have had to fight hard for market share. US institutions, in particular, have not had the overwhelming impact in international private banking within Europe as their investment banking and corporate banking counterparts have had. However, they could be well positioned to improve on this as market demand becomes more oriented towards performance and international investment.

Despite the high levels of competitive activity in Europe, the region still shows all the hallmarks of a relatively unsophisticated market. To date, with a few notable exceptions, there is little refined segmentation and strategies tend to reflect natural strengths of the providers. However, the competitive environment is remarkable for the long dominance of the Swiss commercial banks, the demise of the privately owned Swiss banks and the levelling-out of the competitive playing field.

Dominance of the Swiss commercial banks[5]

Until recently, Swiss commercial banks have been content to rest on their laurels, given the historic lack of competition in international private banking. However, now that the industry is much more competitive and customer driven, the Swiss commercial banks have started to compete more actively. Pressure has also come from within where profitability from the domestic retail banking sector has been poor and is not expected to improve in the short term. This has meant added reliance on major contributors to group profits like international private banking to perform. In contrast to the competition, international private banking has always been a core business for the Swiss commercial banks. The requirement today is to prop up ailing sister business lines. Swiss Bank Corporation expects private banking (and investment banking) to contribute as much as three-quarters of group profits by 1999/2000. Responses to growing competition have been:

- **Pricing:** Until 1990, Swiss providers had operated in a rather gentlemanly way with a pricing cartel that to a great extent stifled competition amongst themselves. Within the industry, Swiss providers have always had the reputation for being expensive in absolute terms as well as in terms of value for money; it was thought that clients were charged a premium for deposit rather than investment management services. A recent report has suggested that this is no longer true.[2]
- **Investment performance:** This has been seen by the industry as the Achilles' heel of the Swiss commercial banks, at least from the non-Swiss private bankers' point of view! As in the case of other providers, there appears to have been a period of upgrading and improvement on how client's assets are managed, with changes in organisational structure; introduction of greater technical and more focused expertise; diversification of asset classes available to investors; and (a

slight) alteration in investment style. In any event, investment house-style can be hard for the client to detect. Private bankers generally will admit to differences not only within centres such as London and Switzerland, but also within the same organisation in various centres. The Swiss house-style may still have a more conservative leaning despite the modified investment approach; however, the reasonable argument still prevails that a more conservative approach has benefits where market volatility is high.

- **Client service model:** The classic servicing model, established by the Swiss private bankers, has largely changed to respond better to the requirements of the private banking marketplace. The long-established service model where the investment manager is also the relationship manager is still evident, particularly in Switzerland because of the preponderance of advisory clients and because of tradition. In some quarters it has been voiced that this multi-faceted role of portfolio-cum-relationship manager has contributed to the view that Swiss service is not always as consistent as it should be. However, this could probably be levelled at some non-Swiss providers too. Swiss providers, particularly those operating out of London, have tended to establish a split-role service model, where each client has a relationship manager and a portfolio manager. Certainly, the potential advantages with regard to up-front servicing of the customer together with focused management of the portfolio are evident in this evolved structure.

- **Product diversification:** Although the Swiss may have lacked product capability in the past when compared with other universal providers, they have made up some ground in the product breadth and depth they can offer. They have acquired Anglo-Saxon trust capability by extending their expertise to common-law trusts set up in the Channel Islands. In addition, in foreign exchange trading, particularly in London, structured products are now more widely available. However, the Swiss banks origins in investment offshore private banking still prevail, despite the fact that they have, within the structure of a universal provider, the potential product fire-power to significantly expand their range of products and services.

Table 4.2 Swiss privately owned banks

Name	Founding date	HQ	Staff
La Roche	1787	Basle	80
Bank Sarasin	1841	Basle	413
E. Gutzwiller	1886	Basle	45
Baumann	1920	Basle	28
Darier Hentsch	1796	Geneva	450
Lombard Odier	1798	Geneva	823
Pictet	1805	Geneva	930
Mirabaud	1819	Geneva	100
Bordier	1844	Geneva	96
Gonet	1845	Geneva	n/a
Mourgue d'Algue	1869	Geneva	n/a
Landolt	1780	Lausanne	n/a
Hentsch Chollet	1882	Lausanne	n/a
Falck[1]	1875	Lucerne	n/a
Wegelin & Co, Inhaber Eugster & Co	1741	St Gallen	n/a
Rahn & Bodmer	1750	Zurich	n/a
Hottinger	1968	Zurich	n/a

[1] On 15 October 1996, Julius Baer Holdings announced the take-over of Falck

Source: The Wernlin Directory, 1995–1996 Private Banking, Asset Management in Switzerland, Gunter Woernle

The demise of the Swiss privately owned banks[6]

Swiss privately owned banks are where the traditions of private banking are rooted. However, many of these banks have disappeared, merged or been acquired, thanks not least to the Swiss commercial banks which went on a spending spree in the early 1990s. Across Europe and primarily in the UK, Switzerland and Germany, there is still a small stable of banks that have resisted incorporation and manage to hold their own in the increasingly competitive environment. But competition has left its mark on the Swiss privately owned banks and only 16 are left.

Whereas competition has done nothing but intensify in private banking in general, there has been an unlikely spirit of co-operation in this diminishing breed of Swiss bank, the five largest partnerships in Geneva having formed their own association. Today, most of them retain their unlimited liability partnership structure and the family is still very much in evidence. The strengths of the privately owned banks most often mentioned by competitors are their partnership structure which fosters employee loyalty and retention, and the fact that they have remained true to their roots of providing their customers with superior and individually tailored services. Some limitations exist today, though, in their product range, ability to lend and international presence. Product shortfalls have been made up by forming alliances with other product providers such as fund management houses and by diversifying into institutional fund management.

On the other hand, Banque Vontobel and Julius Baer Holdings, once privately owned with an unlimited liability structure, have broken away from this tightly knit group and have sought a more secure future by converting to common stock companies. The Baer family has retained 49% of controlling shares and therefore control by the original founding family has been preserved. For Vontobel, there are no family heirs.

It is hard, though, to envisage a rosy future for all of the independently owned banks, given the ever-increasing threat from the well-established global operations of the Swiss commercial banks and US providers such as Citibank and Merrill Lynch. It has been mooted that survival depends on further mergers between the privately owned banks and on forging ties with foreign financial groups, although there is yet to be a precedent for the latter solution. The dialogue between Lombard Odier and US Trust in 1995 did not result in a fruitful alliance. However, of the privately owned stable, whether recently departed or still independent, Pictet, Bank Julius Baer and Darier Hentsch all show strong growth in rises of assets under management, reflecting successful dual strategies targeting niches in international private banking and institutional markets.

An increasingly level competitive playing field[7]

To be as Swiss as possible appears to have been an essential competitive strategy when building an international private bank. This has meant providing a Swiss-style private banking service from Switzerland. The attractiveness of operating out of Switzerland can be seen by the steady growth of foreign-controlled banks in Switzerland from 104 in 1985 to 145 in 1995. The rise in the number of these banks can be largely attributed to international private banking. Further evidence of the success of 'Swissness' can be seen in the size and share of cross-border monies controlled by foreign banks in Switzerland:

- Total asset-management business of foreign banks in Switzerland is estimated at approximately US$ 276 billion for 1994. More than 85% of this on behalf of private investors, most of whom are domiciled abroad.
- The share of fiduciaries of foreign-controlled banks, at the end of 1995, was $90 billion, compared with that of the 'Big Three' (Crédit Suisse, Swiss Bank Corporation, and Union Bank of Switzerland, which had a total of $41 billion. The total level of fiduciary business in Switzerland was $186 billion.
- At the level of individual providers, foreign start-ups have shown strong growth. Merrill Lynch Bank (Suisse) SA has delivered the most substantial growth within its International Private Banking Group for the past few years, with income before taxes and provisions increasing from $23 million in 1995 to $30 million in 1996. Client assets, too, have increased significantly, up from $4.7 billion in 1994 to $6.9 billion in 1996, which suggests that 'Swissness' goes a long way and has levelled-out the competitive playing field.

While the above statistics endorse Switzerland as an attractive destination for cross-border wealth, and the cost of doing business in Switzerland is not such a barrier, it also appears that the foreign banks are becoming increasingly successful in centres which were once the exclusive domain of the Swiss.

Influx of new entrants

There is little indication that the pace of competitor activity in Europe is abating. Some activities have been significant and have reshaped the competitive landscape. Unusually, standing alongside the heavyweights of the global providers, are certain individual banks which can be scene-stealers in the theatre of private banking:

- Merrill Lynch has been one of the most innovative and aggressive providers within Europe, certainly having great foresight in its anticipation of a major regulatory change. Its strategy underwent a major sea-change in response to the 1988 2nd European Banking Directive (passed in December 1989) and it converted its brokerage offices to fully licensed banks and has used this as a market entry strategy to build up its private banking business within Europe.

- New European bank entrants such as the Dutch, including ABN Amro, ING Bank and Rabobank, the second-largest bank in the Netherlands with strong links with the domestic agricultural co-operative sector, have been opening up operations in Luxembourg, Guernsey and Zürich.
- Numerous asset managers, with a dual focus on institutions and hugely wealthy individuals, have entered the market; Robeco, a leading European fund manager, has private banking operations in Geneva and Luxembourg.
- Boutiques such as Soros specialised in fund management can be aggressive competitors for full-service providers when competing head-to-head in a single product category.
- There have been a number of *de novo* operations such as the Greek Latsis family who set up the Private Bank and Trust Co in the early 1990s and, more particularly, Safra Republic Holdings SA, established in 1988 by Edmond Safra, principal shareholder in Republic National Bank of New York, which has grown rapidly from a zero base to $18.4 billion under management as at June 1996, equalling a number of traditional providers. Its strong growth in such a short time, utilising the Safra family-owned banking network, highlights the somewhat stagnant position of some private banking names that can boast a presence in the marketplace of several hundred years. Although the Safra start-up is somewhat untypical, it does highlight the power of reputation in this market and the fact that success can come in comparatively small sizes.

The revival of European competitors

Large European commercial banks such as Lloyds, National Westminster through Coutts, Barclays, Midland, Dresdner and Deutsche Bank have re-invigorated existing operations. The investment has come at a time when domestic private banking is also on the upsurge in home markets, with many of the leading European commercial banks elevating private banking both on the home and international front. However, some, such as Coutts, have been quietly operating in Europe for much of this century, particularly in Switzerland and the Channel Islands.

The revival of possibly languishing operations has come in the form of:

- **Investment in infrastructure:** Examples include Lloyds and Coutts which have both made significant financial investment for the medium term, taking bottom-line hits in 1995 as a result of developing systems, expanding offices and hiring additional people.
- **Embedding acquired private banking operations:** Large-scale acquisitions where private banking units were part of the overall deal have deepened some providers' presence in the marketplace. Dresdner Bank's acquisition of the UK merchant bank Kleinwort Benson has brought the German bank a domestic and international business, particularly in the Middle East. Kleinwort Benson Private Bank will now focus wholly on domestic business within the UK and Dresdner Private Bank will absorb its international business and be the international private bank of the group. The acquisition of Midland by HSBC has given it a small foothold in Switzerland through Guyerzeller Bank, adding to its existing operations, British Bank of the Middle East.

Strategies

Private banking strategies in Europe are no different from strategies in other regions in that there is something of the herd instinct about them. Few providers deviate from the typical worldwide threshold of clients with at least $1 million of investible wealth, except the investment banks that target the top end of wealth, starting at $5 million, and some of the asset managers that will accept subscription rates lower than $1 million.

Growth

Growth is achieved in a number of ways, from organic growth through expansion of outlets and marketing effort to the hiring of account officers with an existing client portfolio. Some institutions, though, have taken more significant steps to increase their market share of private banking wealth through their European operations:

- **Acquisitions of smaller privately owned banks by the 'Big Three':** Crédit Suisse acquired Bank Leu, Bank Clariden and Bank Hoffman; Union Bank of Switzerland acquired Cantrade Private Bank and Hyposwiss; and Swiss Bank

Corporation acquired Armand von Ernst, Bank Ehinger, Adler and Ferrier Lullin in 1992.

- **Acquisitions of smaller privately owned banks by smaller European banks;** for example, Vontobel Holding and Union Banque Privée, which have become larger either through outright acquisitions or by acquiring stakes in other banks to gain market share and entry into other European markets. Vontobel Holding acquired an 80% controlling stake in Bankhaus Berger in Austria; Union Bancaire Privée has expanded through minority stakes in Germany and Scandinavia as well as in the acquisition of Nordfinanza Bank (Zürich). These European expansionist actions also have the effect of protecting them from predators.
- **Expansion of outlets**, typically representative offices, to reflect growing opportunities.

Delivery and distribution

However, overall, international private banking is notoriously selective about its physical presence, maintaining its historically discreet profile. Expansion, though, is as much about new market entry and onshore servicing as about acquiring a presence in a new jurisdiction to enhance products and services.

A minimal European presence generally centres on a core set of locations that reflect a blend of jurisdictions for product vehicles, client servicing and marketing purposes. This set of locations would typically be London, Switzerland, Channel Islands and Luxembourg. Some of the larger providers have additional outlets in Madrid, Frankfurt, Rome, Monaco, Lisbon and Vienna.

The most extensive and rapid expansion has on the whole been by non-European providers such as Citibank and Merrill Lynch, which generally have full service branches rather than representative offices. Citibank has continued to expand in accordance with its global consumer banking strategy; Merrill on the back of its huge US private client franchise, which gives it a distinct advantage as to products, technology, research and execution.

Products and services

Historically, private banking services provided from Europe reflected the dominance of the Swiss, hence the evolution of the Swiss style of private banking and the investment orientation. The Swiss style has long been considered a service to emulate. A focused product range consisting of fiduciary deposits, portfolio management, custody and precious metals has traditionally been supported by the intangible commodities of secrecy and confidentiality. Wealth preservation at any cost, which was the cornerstone of European private banking for much of this century, is a diminishing requirement. Reflecting this, product strategies for most banking providers have largely been based on expansion beyond traditional lines to the point that universal providers look largely similar; with middle-tier providers delivering more and more services, and product specialists remaining specialised and competing with universal providers on depth and expertise on a single-product basis.

Expansion reflects product advancements in the capital markets and the shift of customer demand towards a more international investment orientation, better performance and a more composite approach to total wealth management, including estate and tax planning. Property investments also feature, responding to demand from Hong Kong, Singapore and the Middle East.

Regulation and legislation

One of the characteristics of the regulatory and legislative environment in Europe is the increasing move away from a national to a more international focus, acknowledging the global nature of banking. Drivers come from both within and outside the European boundaries.

Bank for international settlements (BIS)

The Basle Committee on Banking Supervision and the Offshore Group of Banking Supervisors have both stated their shared aim to strengthen cross-border banking supervision. The proposals would include a recommendation to lift the bank secrecy laws for the purpose of cross-border on-site inspections by home country supervisors. Their main aim is to improve international banking practices and curb money-laundering activities through enhanced information flows between regulatory bodies.

To bring this into effect, regulations would have to be changed within local jurisdictions. This undoubtedly conflicts with current regulations in place in some jurisdictions.

Banking confidentiality and the Swiss[8]

The Swiss are facing the strongest attack on their reputation for probity for decades. Allegations about Nazi gold and about Swiss banks sitting on billions of dollars belonging to the survivors of Holocaust victims are provoking debate about how tightly Switzerland is regulated as a financial centre. However, it seems only a matter of time before Switzerland will meet an international minimum standard required to combat money laundering, despite the arguments from some quarters that the voluntary due diligence code of conduct that binds Swiss banks, introduced in 1977, is sufficient. For purposes of the investigation into assets deposited in Switzerland during the Second World War, banking secrecy will be suspended.

Under Swiss civil law, a banker is obliged to keep absolute secrecy regarding information relating to customers, thereby observing the bank's duty to confidentiality and the customer's right to privacy. In Swiss law, to have omitted to declare part of one's financial position does not constitute a criminal offence and cannot therefore be the object of judicial assistance. However, in the case of tax fraud that involves deception of the tax authorities, for example by the use of forged documents, judicial assistance in criminal matters can be granted to a foreign authority.

The anticipated new Money Laundering Bill would apply to both the banking and non-banking communities including money managers, credit card providers and currency traders. In addition, the proposed law would make the reporting of dubious accounts a legal obligation for all financial intermediaries.

What appears to be taking place in Switzerland today is what hitherto would have been described as the 'reconciling the irreconcilable'. That is, complying with Swiss sovereign law and the duty of banking confidentiality at the same time as bowing to mounting international pressure to address more forcefully the problem of international financial crime in the spirit of teamwork. Ironically, though, pressure to conform comes not just from the international arena, but also from within Switzerland, where the chief proponent of change has been the Swiss federal prosecutor.

In the past, Switzerland has made some amendments to its legislation to support the prosecution authorities and signed bilateral treaties with a number of countries including the USA, Canada and Australia. However, this is all symptomatic of the greater issue of Switzerland becoming more involved internationally and abandoning its historical position of neutrality.

The draft Swiss money-laundering bill, because it addresses both banks and non-banks, will therefore be a complex piece of legislation. The bill is not expected to be passed before 1998, particularly given Switzerland's populist approach to passing laws.

European Union[9]

The EU is extending its influence over the financial services operating environment within its member countries. It is undoubtedly contributing to the growing transparency of wealth; whether this is entirely welcomed by either providers or clients is another matter. It is also addressing the problem of unevenness of the playing field within the member countries as well as of that on which both members and non-member countries compete.

The issues which relate to the EU are not wholly exclusive to private banking, but are common to all financial services institutions operating within the EU.

- **Banking confidentiality:** Banks in Europe are increasingly concerned about the threat of government agencies making inroads into banking confidentiality - and not just foreign governments but the national governments too. Concerns revolve around the long-standing duty to maintain privacy over a customer's affairs and the onus on the bank official whose behaviour is now judged by criminal law. The German tax authorities have already demonstrated that banking confidentiality is no longer sacrosanct: raids were made on premises of Dresdner Bank in pursuit of evidence of tax evasion, as well as on Commerzbank's Luxembourg subsidiary.
- **European single currency:** While the prospects for monetary union remain plagued by uncertainty, what is certain is that a single currency will have an impact both on the private banking providers and on the clients. Client choice is likely to be affected, with a possible revenue re-balancing, giving fewer currency options. Providers will have to be prepared to convert in time and without disruption to the client in areas such as cross-border payments, settlement, trading conventions, denomination of securities and reporting.
- **Tax harmonisation:** One of the current debates is that surrounding the harmonisation of withholding tax and the establishment of a common approach to levying the tax.

Germany is the most vociferous country, demanding uniformity across member countries. However, the application of a uniform approach extends the argument beyond the EU and into the OECD. Luxembourg is highly resistant to EU uniformity since it competes with Switzerland for funds and currently is at an advantage in not levying withholding tax. A precedent has been set, because value-added tax is already subject to harmonising rules, though members can set their own rates within wide bands. However, the European Commission has conceded that it is feasible that policies relating to taxation, particularly harmonised taxation, might be incorporated in the EMU.

- **Money laundering:** The EU has already ring-fenced banks of member states, which are obliged to report all suspicious cases of money laundering on a mandatory basis. Member countries are already tightening up domestic laws. In the UK, the Criminal Justice Act (1993) includes provisions that make substantial changes to present legislation on money laundering. It is now an offence for any person to fail to report any knowledge or suspicion, acquired in the course of business on behalf of the person or the person's employer, of the laundering of drug trafficking or terrorist monies. Furthermore, it is now an offence to become involved in or assist in any transaction which a person suspects is connected with laundering the proceeds of any crime.

For some countries in the EU, new directives could be a way of eliminating previous weaknesses, particularly those relating to taxation. However, the overall issue of tax competition across jurisdictions is now on the international agenda.

Conclusions and outlook

Europe will continue to be the dominant region for international private banking, given its position as the largest manager of worldwide cross-border wealth and as the largest regional source of cross-border wealth. While remaining attractive for clients, particularly non-European clients, it will also continue to be a highly competitive area for providers, both as a centre for non-European wealth and for cross-border wealth within Europe. It probably represents one of the toughest private banking regions, given the dual forces of competitive intensity and margin erosion.

Opportunities are as much about the increasing wealth of existing clients as about taking clients from the competition and developing clients in markets where new wealth creation is at the fore. The main drivers for European wealth to cross borders are usually a desire for greater international diversification and the search for a more benign tax environment and these drivers are likely to endure for sometime.

Competition from Europe-based providers is now a much more open race, with the narrowing of the gap between Swiss and non-Swiss providers. US providers in particular should continue to make inroads into European wealth, with the market moving towards more of an international investment and performance orientation. Moreover, they have a more aggressive, new-business-driven culture and a range of quality, well-executed services such as US dollar products, structured products and broking services, which should be key factors contributing to their success. it is likely that the privately owned Swiss banks will reduce further in number through mergers and acquisitions and the competitive landscape will continue to be fragmented.

While confidentiality, particularly that offered by the likes of Switzerland, Liechtenstein and Austria, will continue to be bought as a product, asset-management services will be at the core of propositions offered to international private banking clients within Europe, in keeping with services in other regions. International pressure will tilt the Swiss more towards conformity and, although not a member of the EU, Switzerland will be increasingly sensitive to its worldwide position, particularly with regard to Jewish money deposited in Switzerland during the Second World War, an issue that will take several years to resolve.

Significant expansion of international private banking outlets is not expected and servicing will continue to be out of the main international centres such as London and Switzerland.

The EU, in keeping with today's growing tide of international cooperation and regulation, will continue to bind financial services operators through directives applicable to all EU members. Complex issues such as the harmonisation of taxes and the OECD review of unfair competition will be hard to resolve in the short term and are expected to be an enduring item on the European (and international) agenda for some time.

Notes

1 *World Wealth Report 1997*, Gemini Consulting and Merrill Lynch.
2 Crédit Suisse First Boston, January 1997.
3 *London Stock Exchange Fact Book 1996*. The annual direct cost of financing the regulators' activities in Britain was $140 million (compared with $795 million in the USA). Survey: International Banking, *The Economist*, 27 April 1996.
4 Edward P.M. Gardener and Philip Molyneux, *Changes in Western European Banking*, 1990, p. 136.
5 'Big Three have expanded', Survey: Swiss Banking, *Financial Times*, 28 October 1996.
6 'Togetherness, Swiss Private Banks', *The Economist*, 19 October 1996, p. 131.
7 Association of Foreign Banks in Switzerland, Annual Report 1995/1996; Swiss Banking Commission (verbal communication); Merrill Lynch Bank (Suisse) SA Annual Report 1995.
8 'Buffeted by stormy seas of change', Survey: Swiss Banking, *Financial Times*, 28 October 1996; 'Keeping mum', *The Economist*, 17 February 1996; 'Swiss Banking Secrecy and International Co-operation', *Global Private Banking*, 15 April 1996, p. 12, 'The Swiss Money Laundering Bill', *Global Private Banking*, 22 July 1996, p. 12; 'Switzerland and the Jews', *The Economist*, 11 May 1996.

   There are currently great tensions between governments and banks as to respective role and responsibilities. Most recently, in Europe, Dresdner Bank and Commerzbank both experienced raids on their premises. This led Dresdner Bank to criticise openly the German tax authorities and accuse them of using the banks to police an unworkable system.
9 'Europe's flexible friends', *The Economist*, 18 January 1997, p. 58.

CHAPTER FIVE

The Americas

Introduction

North America and Latin America need to be looked at together in the international private banking context. The USA in particular is closely linked with Latin America where both politically and economically its influence is deeply felt. However, the markets are very different. Given that the US dollar is the leading global currency, the wealthy US investor has been provided with stability and little incentive to invest in multi-currencies. Given recent stock market performance in the USA, particularly in 1996, it would not have made sense to have shifted wealth cross-border either for investment performance. Although there has been a domestic orientation of investment attitudes, there are signs of increased equity diversification under-way. Much of the US wealth that is placed offshore goes to the Cayman Islands but typically monies are re-invested in dollars within the USA often using fiduciary services. The main reasons for going offshore are connected with tax avoidance through the use of trusts, or with international trade and foreign businesses. However, some would argue that there are disincentives for US wealth going offshore, not least the tax on worldwide sources of income.

It is Latin America that is more central to the opportunity today and more in keeping with the traditional evolution of international private banking services. Three major changes have characterised Latin

America since the 1980s: the end of dictatorships, the end of hyperinflation and the start of growth in foreign investment. With a new generation of foreign-educated leaders, financial liberalisation and trade reform have been instrumental in changing the economic and political landscape of the region.

It was to the USA and foreign institutions that wealthy Latin Americans turned in order to protect their wealth. Flight capital and a safe haven deposit with a bank in the USA were typical of the 1970s and 1980s. However, with a new generation of wealth developers, a second generation of wealth builders and a number of leading emerging market economies within the region, international private banking services are shifting into another gear. For many, the days of asset protection alone are over and the days of formal financial planning are beginning. However, the US influence is by no means diminishing, with providers such as Citibank and Merrill Lynch making emerging markets within Latin America their area of specialisation.

Wealth and the wealthy

In 1996, total high net worth assets in Latin America were estimated at $2.2 trillion, which is 13% of worldwide wealth, and is up from an estimated $1.2 trillion in 1986.[1] However, as in Africa and the Middle East, wealth within Latin America is still characteristically held by a tiny proportion of the population.

Markets

Overall, Latin America has been showing strong economic growth; OECD forecasts are predicting an average 4% growth in 1997, an enviable rate compared with that of many European economies. However, the sustained growth found in some of the Asian countries has proved elusive for many Latin American markets. The larger and more accessible private banking markets within Latin America have been identified as Argentina, Brazil, Chile and Mexico.

- **Argentina:** The days of 7% heady growth between 1991 and 1994 have been followed by a recession, largely as a result of the Mexico financial crisis of 1994–95; economic growth was expected to be about 4% in 1997. Some consider Argentina one of the more highly competitive markets and international private bankers have been marketing there for some time.

- **Brazil:** Brazil has the largest economy and the largest population. Its privatisation programme, rather low profile to date, should move up a gear with sell-offs within the transport and utilities industries. Economic growth in 1997 was expected to be about 4%, a step up from 1996.
- **Chile:** Considered by many to be at the vanguard of Latin American social, political and economic reform, Chile continues to lead on economic performance, with OECD forecasts of economic growth around 5–6%. Despite a slow down in growth, it should continue to be the best-performing economy in the region. Like Argentina, it is considered to be one of the more competitive international private banking markets.
- **Mexico:** Set to grow at about 5% in 1997, Mexico is the region's second-fastest-growing economy.

Colombia, Venezuela and Peru have been identified as international private banking markets on a smaller scale.

Drivers of cross-border wealth

It is probably Latin America more than any other region that has dominated worldwide banking history recently. Third World debt and the inability to pay back international loans have made their mark on most world-class banking organisations. What has typified this period of history has been the huge amounts of flight capital that left the region. During the period 1983–85, significant amounts of wealth left Mexico, Argentina and Venezuela. Although repatriation has taken place and continues to take place, it is still considered only a fraction of the original outflow, given the increase in asset values.[2] Contributing to flight capital were the military dictatorships and the lack of democratic process, instability in the banking sector and economic volatility.

Repatriation of capital has been a response to both incentives within the region and external factors. The incentives within Latin America have been political reform, economic growth, development of the financial markets and privatisation of state-owned companies. Assisting repatriation further has been the fall of US interest rates in the early 1990s. The added icing on the cake were some specific government incentives relating to tax evasion; a notable example was in Argentina where penalties were lifted and an extensive advertising campaign was carried out to encourage Argentinians to bring their private wealth back.

With a strong desire to invest locally, the holders of repatriated wealth typically have invested in dollar-denominated Latin American paper, often in nominee name, an extra safeguard for tax purposes. With the growth of the capital markets, there has also been investment in privatisation issues, the more tangible and visible institutions such as Telefonica Argentina often being favoured.

International private bankers still believe that the continuing key to attracting wealth back to the local economy is local instruments, given the strong and continuing desire by wealthy Latin Americans to invest locally. Although the US dollar still prevails, it is no longer the only currency in which Latin Americans will invest.

The wealthy

As with private wealth from Asia, private bankers make a definite distinction between old and new wealth. As in Europe, wealth has traditionally been in the hands of the very few and has been passed down in the form of land, property and family businesses. New wealth, on the other hand, has been achieved through commerce with the advent of a new generation of entrepreneurs, often foreign educated, and with an outlook that is strikingly similar to that of their Asian counterparts.

Needs of the wealthy

To understand the needs of Latin American wealthy individuals, it is important to appreciate how enduring the highly volatile economic context has been. The needs of the wealthy have been shaped largely by the economic and political instability of the region, creating an overwhelming requirement for asset protection. With stability collapsing during the 1970s and 1980s, the main way of ensuring protection of family wealth was to deposit it in the USA or in Switzerland. On the whole though, with the overriding priority being to find a secure haven it was normally only felt necessary to get the money out of the region (allegedly through exchange houses), and to deposit the money in a bank account in the USA, usually in the investor's own name. Depositing within the USA combined the physical safety of assets and currency protection, while local currencies were being ravaged by high volatility and soaring inflation.

The dollar orientation has become almost the habit of a lifetime, even though a more sophisticated approach to portfolio diversification would make greater sense. The concept of total wealth management is only recently becoming accepted and it continues to be dogged by a desire to avoid tax and a fear of recurring instability, both economic and political. The legacy of the past manifests itself today in some of the largely unmet needs which relate to estate planning and protection; the favouring of nominal over real returns and using local interest rates against which to judge the performance of international equities and as the basis of investment decision making. Despite this, needs are significantly more diverse these days. Some private bankers believe it is a performance-based relationship, requiring active global asset management, and that the capital preservation days are over. However, other private bankers still see a divergence of needs, with the older wealthy looking for conservative international investment to safeguard their assets, whereas the younger generation is looking for aggressive investment growth, both in the local investment market and internationally. Undoubtedly first-generation international entrepreneurs have a distinctive set of needs over and above private wealth management.

For the new generation of wealthy, particularly those who are increasingly influenced by foreign education and an international lifestyle, the priorities today and increasingly for the future relate to estate planning, business planning and active asset management. This reflects the very real and important transition from flight capital to financial planning in line with economic and business trends:

- **Estate planning:** With growing signs that governments are addressing the problems of fiscal deficit, it is no longer a question of if, but rather when, the tax authorities will catch up with flagrant tax evasion, allegedly rife in the old days and still widespread today. A change of heart is becoming detectable among international private banking clients, who are increasingly turning to formal tax planning, which requires, for example, the use of trusts and legal structures. This indicates a growing acceptance of, or at least resignation to, the issues of payment of personal taxes and a need to plan ahead formally.
- **Business planning:** By no means alone, entrepreneurs in Latin America have been facing head-on a number of issues relating to business planning such as succession within the company, particularly in family businesses, and to development plans for the business itself, particularly in the context of flotations, foreign investment and outward-looking economies.
- **Active asset management:** This will continue to be one of

the key thrusts of international private banking and certainly the key to attracting further repatriated funds. For many international private bankers, the challenge is to provide local products and to deliver performance that compares favourably with returns obtainable on repatriated funds invested in domestic products. A further challenge will be to ensure that the portfolio is properly diversified, trying to wean investors away from over-investment in the US dollar as well as getting them to recognise that portfolio management is about a long-term approach rather than timing the market.

Financial centres within the Americas

Latin American wealth typically moves in a number of directions to destinations that are local, regional or in other parts of the world. The strong affinities that Latin Americans have for certain wealth destinations have as much to do with historical and cultural associations as with faith in the particular centre's stability and economic outlook.

The influence that the USA has on Latin America is not just political. For some time, the USA has represented the epitome of economic stability; its added and more practical advantage, compared with Europe, is its geographic proximity and the sharing of time zones. All this explains why New York and Miami in particular have become significant servicing centres for wealth from Latin America.

However, notwithstanding the importance of the USA and also of Europe, Uruguay has consistently been an important regional destination for private wealth originating from Latin America.

Uruguay

Uruguay is the only jurisdiction in Latin America that qualifies as a tax haven and is one of the few financial centres in the world where Spanish is the primary language. Within Latin America, Uruguay historically has been less volatile than its neighbours and has therefore been a safe haven for a proportion of the region's flight capital as well as a platform for trade and investment into Argentina and Brazil. Like Switzerland, Uruguay has had its fair share of stories about money-filled suitcases crossing its border. Furthermore, Uruguay is not hesitant in stating that its banking secrecy laws are stronger than Switzerland's.

While Uruguay has undoubtedly taken action to develop its infrastructure, particularly with pension funds and local capital markets, it is still considered a relatively unsophisticated financial centre. Its genuine strengths are more in the banking sector where deposits, current accounts and certificates of deposits are the order of the day.

Stability of centre is all important and Uruguay has had stable banking laws underpinning its overall attractiveness, in stark contrast to neighbouring countries where, overnight, banking laws have changed and assets been frozen or devalued.

Foreign banks control virtually all of Uruguay's private banking sector and this is an additional safeguard for Latin American clients.

Concerns have been voiced that Uruguay's advantages as an offshore centre could be eroded as banking legislation within Argentina and Brazil catches up.[3]

Panama

Until 1986, Panama was another regional financial centre for wealth originating from Latin America. However, despite the overthrow of the Noriega government, Panama is no longer considered reputable as an international financial centre. The recovery of its reputation is still some way off the horizon although attempts are being made to rebuild it as an international centre. However, Panama is not helping its case by turning down a US request to extradite an alleged money launderer, accused of recycling $500 million.[4]

Financial centres within the USA

New York

Like London, New York represents for the wealthy a sophisticated financial centre where there is a wide range of US providers, from money managers and brokers to banks, and an extensive selection of dollar-denominated products available, and where competition is intense.

Miami

Miami tends to act as both the gateway to the USA and the stepping stone to Latin America. It is a highly hispanicised city and, together with New York, is one of the main centres with Latin America as its primary target. The financial community has flourished, with Edge Act institutions where the licence restricts the provider to offering offshore services only to non-US residents. Many of these local institutions in Miami have offices in the Cayman Islands, Bahamas or Uruguay to attract wealthy individuals who prefer to invest locally through offshore branches for tax reasons.

Other financial centres within the Caribbean and Central America

Caribbean islands, seeking to diversify their normally limited sources of economic growth, have not been slow to realise the potential of developing a financial services infrastructure. However, given the proximity of the Caribbean centres to the USA, the latter probably exerts a disproportionately strong influence, particularly in relation to drugs and money laundering. Many islands have responded to US pressure to tighten up on offshore banking regulation, most recently Montserrat and the Cayman Islands.

- **The Cayman Islands**[4]: This is a British Crown Colony with more than 560 trust companies and banks including 47 of the world's top 50 banks, deposits from these institutions collectively exceeding $500 billion. More than 370 insurance companies are based in the Cayman Islands, as are 900 mutual funds with a net asset value of $39 billion. It has also been estimated that there are 32,000 offshore companies, many of them from Asia.

  The reputation of the Cayman Islands has been undeniably mixed: so much so, that in 1995, its regulatory system was subject to an audit by the Caribbean Financial Action Task Force. This is part of the International Financial Action Task Force, set up by the G7 countries to implement the Vienna Convention against traffic in drugs.

  Notably, the Cayman Islands have tightened up in a number of areas including the Bank and Companies Law (1983) which has been amended to allow mutual sharing of information between jurisdictions. The Cayman Islands are now more aligned with the international arena. Whether this has completely dispelled the Cayman Island's reputation for money laundering is another matter.

Smaller centres include:

- **Antigua:** Recently, it has begun to earn the reputation for alleged money laundering activities in connection with wealth sourced from Russian and drugs from Colombia, despite protestations to the contrary by the government. Under both

British and US pressure, agreement has been reached to curb drug trafficking and money laundering; amendments to the existing law are expected.

- **The Bahamas:** Like the Cayman Islands, The Bahamas is one of the leading centres in the Caribbean where banking, investment, trust and fiduciary services are provided to both individuals and corporate clients. It is also an attractive domicile for shipping companies, various managed companies and banks.
- **Bermuda:** Unsurprisingly, as Britain's oldest colony, Bermuda has a legal system similar to the UK's. With low-tax status, its financial services sector accounts for some 40% of revenue. However, it is more renowned for its captive commercial insurance firms. It has a good reputation for financial integrity and has attracted a number of head offices to be domiciled there, most notably Jardine Matheson which moved its headquarters there in 1984. It has been estimated that a further 260 Hong Kong companies have also moved their official headquarters to Bermuda.
- **British Virgin Islands (BVI):** This is a British colony with about 180,000 offshore companies registered. It has strengthened its focus on offshore corporate registration, particularly since the fall from grace of Panama. Like the Cayman Islands, BVI have been at the receiving end of US attention; so much so, that in 1984, the USA terminated its double-taxation treaty with BVI as part of a general sweep against tax evasion by American citizens.
- **Dutch Antilles:** It comes within the jurisdiction of the EU. Given its geographic proximity, it has been attractive to monies from Venezuela, but probably it is most renowned for the George Soros funds domiciled in its jurisdiction.
- **Turks and Caicos Islands:** This is one of the least-developed British dependencies in the Caribbean and a tax haven with no taxes on income, capital gains, corporate profits, inheritances or estates. Its governor has recently been quoted as saying that Turks and Caicos suffers from rampant drug trafficking, official corruption, high unemployment and incompetent police. In 1985 its chief minister and two other government officials were jailed for allowing illicit drugs into the islands.

Other centres include Barbados, Anguilla, Montserrat and the US Virgin Islands.

Table 5.1 Notable international private banking

US banks	Chase Manhattan Bank, Citibank, Bank of Boston
Swiss commercial banks	Union Bank of Switzerland, Crédit Suisse, Swiss Bank Corporation
US investment banks	Goldman Sachs, JP Morgan, Merrill Lynch
European banks	Coutts, Safra Republic, ABN Amro

However, despite the range of centres available within the Caribbean and the USA, significant amounts of Latin American wealth are also destined for Europe, particularly Switzerland, Channel Islands and London.

Competitive environment

The competitive environment is remarkable for the dominance of US providers, the absence of strong domestic competition and the Swiss who continue to operate in the traditional arm's-length way. Added to these dynamics are the important positions of Miami and New York which make the competitive environment a strongly US affair. As in Europe, the competitive arena can look somewhat eclectic, with well-recognised global names and a swarm of small, often single-product providers, which can compete with the universal providers and undoubtedly are attractive to wealthy Latin Americans who thus have a number of providers for different aspects of their overall portfolio.

Some leading international private banking, providers are listed in Table 5.1. In addition, there are large numbers of boutiques, asset managers and fund managers based in Miami and New York.

Dominance of US providers[5]

Undoubtedly, the affinity that the Latin American wealthy have for the dollar plays into the hands of US providers, who typically would have the range of dollar products. With the proximity of the USA and the tendency of wealthy Latin Americans to travel frequently and have a home there, providers can also compete outside the region without having to venture too far afield. However, some of the larger US providers have set up shop in Latin America and this gives them a strong competitive edge.

- Citibank has to be credited with staying power and it has made a virtue of being one of the first to have a presence in Latin America. With 80 years in Brazil and Uruguay, 75 years in Peru and 35 years in Ecuador, it has stayed through thick and thin in Latin America (and elsewhere) despite problems both at home and in the USA: at home in the USA, with crises in the 1980s, culminating in 1991, when the share price dropped to $8.50 with rumours of impending collapse, and in Latin America where the region was lurching from one crisis to another. In the view of some private bankers, commitment to the market and staying power have certainly paid off, in that Citibank have an unequalled market franchise (both consumer and commercial banking) from which to foster international private banking business, as well as an established name for providing services to wealthy families and the next generation.
- The US investment banks, particularly the top-notch firms of JP Morgan and Goldman Sachs, continue to demonstrate their ability to provide a private banking service on a global dimension. Their focus away from their home market is as much to do with lack of opportunity at home as with opportunity abroad. With intense competition in the investment banking scene in the USA, Latin America has seemed an attractive market, given the capital markets development, the almost universal privatisation programmes and the growing number of foreign investors in privatisation issues. International private banking is a neat, and possibly less risky, adjunct to their core business and certainly the investment banks make a splash with the super-wealthy in Latin America.
- Merrill Lynch, in a similar vein to Citibank, has utilised one of its core businesses, investment banking, to develop an international private banking business in Latin America. Unlike the Swiss, but in keeping with Citibank, the approach has been to establish full-service branches. Merrill Lynch has set itself up as an emerging market specialist and Latin America represents one of its most substantial regions for client assets, which total about $18 billion, some 35–40% of its total client assets.

Absence of domestic providers[6]

Latin American banks are going through a similar consolidation phase as Western banks. However, bank failures have been somewhat commonplace notably in Argentina and Venezuela. In 1995, Venezuela's financial services sector lost 17 local privately owned banks. The rest remain under state control and face the rigours of economic reform and stricter regulation. For many domestic providers, there is enough going on in their own backyard to contend with, without entering the area of international private banking, where competition is fierce and where their own capability fades by comparison with that of foreign providers. However, there is some evidence that local banks are recognising the opportunity and see room for themselves in the competitor arena. Developments focus on:

- Establishing an offshore capability in their own right, typically in Uruguay, the Cayman Islands, The Bahamas and Miami.
- Building an in-house range of offshore mutual funds, taking advantage of regulatory developments and loosening of foreign exchange restrictions.
- Seeking alliances with providers which can complement the offering and provide offshore services, for example, from their US branches.

Additionally, local banks are astutely taking advantage of local conditions such as the withholding tax in Ecuador and offering offshore funds where withholding tax does not apply. Domestic providers are reacting quickly to changed legislation and recognising the demand from their customers. While their growth may be high, given the small starting base, it is unrealistic today to think that they are significant thorns in the side of the larger and more experienced foreign providers.

Competitors at arm's-length

The servicing conundrum goes a bit like this: does Mohammed go to the mountain, or does the mountain go to Mohammad? Certainly, in the past, it was the latter, where wealthy Latin Americans sought out services provided by Swiss private bankers. Recognising the growing stability in Latin America and the needs of the wealthy, especially the old wealthy, some of the Swiss in particular have established a level of representation on the ground. Some of the larger Swiss providers have coverage in the form of representative offices, at least, in major capitals.

The Swiss commercial banks use New York (or Miami) as a servicing stepping stone to Latin America. But the commitment shown by the US providers is in stark contrast. While remote servicing was the only choice in the past when money had fled from instability, the remote servicing and scant representation locally today seems out of kilter with new and growing markets and changing service requirements.

Why the difference? The reasons might range from lack of appetite for committing capital to the region (given recent history), to the belief that their clients prefer the 'out of sight out of mind' approach to service, and perhaps a less aggressive attitude to distribution. Or possibly, the break with tradition would be too much in a region that is so far from Switzerland, the control point of the Swiss banks? For some clients, service provided from a representative office, backed up by frequent visits to the region, is acceptable. However, in the long term, with changed needs and the growth of new wealth, it may be that the strength of the brand name will not be enough to still attract new wealth and that changes to their *modus operandi* will be unavoidable.

Alternatively, operating at arm's-length can also be part of a strategy such as marketing non-resident aliens from within the USA. Much of the more recent competitive activity is linked to changing economic fortunes: the fall in US interest rates in the early 1990s, repatriation, the development of the equity markets at home and the corresponding growing equity appetite of Latin American investors. However, one of the key ways of gaining access to international wealth is to market from within the USA, targeting non-resident aliens who are so defined by residing in the USA for less than the maximum period allowed (approximately six months) to avoid payment of US taxes. Latin Americans are not the only non-resident opportunity within the USA but are a major one, which means that a broad range of US provider types are addressing this market, including Citibank and Chase Manhattan; super-regional banks, especially the larger ones in their domestic region such as Barnett Bank in Florida and Wells Fargo in California; and European international private banks such as the Swiss providers and Coutts. Additionally, a unique set of competitors are the Miami boutiques which are often Edge Act institutions. They offer specialised products such as Latin American debt and equity products for Latin American companies and governments. This appeals to Latin American investors looking for higher returns than those obtainable from traditional, more conservative deposit products. While Miami is a key location for clients from Latin America, operations in California and Texas also reflect the market opportunity. Marketing teams will often travel to the home countries of non-resident Latin Americans;

alternatively wealthy Latin Americans will have residences in the USA and are frequent visitors.

Coutts has taken a step away from its European cousins and is actively targeting the emerging markets of Latin America. Like the Swiss providers, Coutts has made camp in the USA with the barest representation in Latin America: an office in Montevideo (which is closing down) and a small representative office in Buenos Aires. Having rejected on-the-ground presence in the region, instead it is building up its cadre of international private bankers, putting more people in place. Coutts has regrouped and operates out of the USA in New York, Miami and San Diego, Los Angeles and Beverley Hills.

Strategies

Few providers deviate from the worldwide typical threshold of clients with at least $1 million of investible wealth, except the investment banks, which target the top end of wealth starting at $5 million and some of the asset managers which will accept subscription rates lower than $1 million.

Growth

Strategies for business expansion remain formulaic with growth plans pursued along organic lines such as office expansion, developing marketing presence and hiring more people. Market entry strategies reinforce the use of core businesses to gain an initial foothold in the private banking market; examples of this are Citibank with its consumer and commercial banking operations and Merrill Lynch with its broking heritage.

Provider strategies to support growth include:

- Establishing a US centre such as Miami or New York to co-ordinate the regional activities.
- Establishing in-country market managers (aka Merrill Lynch) who market and manage locally.
- Controlling the prospecting through local operations while using marketing managers from offshore centres such as London and Switzerland.
- Marketing from Switzerland and London and operating more as lone wolves, with loose association with local operations.

Still prevalent today throughout international private banking and typified in Latin America (though not exclusively there) is the way in which members of different onshore and offshore areas of the same organisation gather in the region. For example, representatives of the same organisation from New York, London and Switzerland can all be marketing their services within the region. On the face of it, this must create problems of control and territory. Some organisations have not left marketing alone to the entrepreneurial talents of the international private banker, and have created roles, remuneration, accounting and organisational structure to facilitate the focus specifically on business development and thus to eliminate internal strife.

Acquisitions are rare but the second part of Swiss Bank Corporation's acquisition plan in 1996 involved the purchase of a $1 billion portfolio of accounts (also including the relationship managers) from Chase Manhattan. Account management was being carried out in New York and Miami, and it therefore strengthened the Swiss provider's presence in the Americas.

Delivery and distribution

Different approaches are clearly evident in Latin America and vary from a country-by-country presence, as in the case of Citibank, to the more minimalist approach shown largely by the Swiss, with only a splattering of representative offices. The most extensive presence, as exemplified by Citibank, would be the major capital cities such as Buenos Aires and São Paolo but also Rio de Janeiro, Santiago, Mexico City, Montevideo, Lima and Caracas.

In keeping with their strategies worldwide, the likes of Merrill Lynch and Citibank provide onshore servicing, anticipating a demand for advisory services.

Products and services

The products and service evolution has shifted from wealth preservation at any cost to a more middle ground of offshore and onshore services, with the beginnings of a growing receptivity to total wealth management and to more international investment diversification. Product-hook strategies have evolved, too, broadening out the products and services to meet the changing needs of wealthy individuals. With changed interest rates offshore, foreign providers are being spurred on by the high rates available locally from local institutions.

There are four discernible products and service routes, suggesting that Latin Americans, like most wealthy individuals, have multiple relationships and compartmentalise their wealth:

- Formal financial planning involving estate planning, business planning and active portfolio management.
- International banking, given that Latin Americans are great travellers not only to the USA but also to Europe - perhaps an advantage for the larger providers which can provide banking services worldwide to clients.
- Local portfolio for comfort and high returns, particularly given some current economic performances.
- A punting portfolio where more risky products such as emerging funds and derivatives might be acquired; Latin Americans also appear to be great collectors of mutual funds.

Regulatory and legislative environment[7]

To some extent, the USA, particularly through its Securities and Exchange Commission, has influenced the banking regulatory framework. This is not surprising, given that many of the new generation of government ministers have been educated in the States, together with the overall influence that the USA has exerted over Latin America.

The regulatory and legislative environment is one of reform and will continue to be so for the foreseeable future. The key areas of reform are described below.

Taxation

Because of the large fiscal deficits in a number of countries, there has been a decisive move by governments to become more efficient in collecting taxes, with measures that have included:

- Simplifying and reducing the personal tax burden.
- Revenue services upgrading their information technology to build up automated histories of tax payers.
- Extension of information links through information exchange provisions in tax treaties to aid identification of tax evaders.
- Providing tax amnesties.

- Reduction in top rates of personal taxes.

Tax reforms in Brazil and Argentina have been notable for reductions of the marginal rate and the simplification of tax bands.

Foreign exchange and capital movements

Elimination of restrictions in all but a few cases has taken place with Brazil leading the way in 1991 and 1992. However, in some markets, for example, Venezuela, restrictions still prevail.

Corruption

Both national and international agendas reflect the growing need to address corruption. With the spectacular case involving Raúl, the brother of ex-President Carlos Salinas of Mexico and the ex-President himself, even a government minister has described the political system in Mexico, where the current ruling party (the Partido Revolucionario Institucional - PRI) has been in power for almost 70 years, as '80% corrupt'.

Capital markets

Extensive legislation has been passed to privatise state-owned firms, encourage inward foreign investment, open up capital markets with the growth of pension funds, and develop the range of financial instruments and the scope of permissible investment both domestically and internationally.

Banking sector

The unstable banking sectors are being reformed through tighter regulation, sales and closures. With a history of government-owned banks and government bail-outs, banking collapses have been seen in Venezuela, Argentina and Mexico. Structural reforms and privatisation of state-owned banks are some of the courses of action on the political agenda.

Conclusions and outlook

The shift from dictatorship to democracy and from closed economies to free-market economies and the rapid development of local capital markets have been instrumental in the development of wealth and international private banking in the region of Latin America. Undoubtedly, the USA has been the chief protagonist from a political, economic and international private banking provider perspective.

The days of asset protection as the central international private banking proposition are coming to an end although still there is affinity for the US dollar, Uruguay and Switzerland, particularly where old money is concerned. There is a detectable shift to a more globally diversified approach to wealth management, but local performance will continue to be an attraction, with the promise of short-term returns.

Key international private banking markets remain Mexico, Brazil, Chile and Argentina - the larger countries, which are at the forefront of Latin America's economic revival. Chile and Argentina, given their more consistent economic performance, could be considered as more competitively saturated than the other markets. Markets waiting to be opened up for international private banking services are Peru, Venezuela and Colombia.

Repatriation of wealth is a characteristic of the 1990s. However, given the rise in asset values, it is still thought that significant amounts of wealth remain offshore. Further repatriation will depend on greater stability within the region that still suffers from degrees of economic instability, civil unrest, terrorist and guerrilla activities, shaky banking systems, corruption and some political instability.

New wealth is characteristic of the region together with the advent of the entrepreneur and, more remarkably, the international entrepreneur, who has a pivotal role in taking forward family owned, or once family owned businesses.

Needs have evolved significantly beyond the panic-stricken days of the 1970s and 1980s to the more stable and liberal times of the 1990s. While the US dollar prevails as a dominant currency, competition has developed, with local products offering highly competitive returns. A Latin American eye is still kept firmly on nominal rates of return despite high inflation in a number of domestic economies. For the wealthy today, the priorities should be (and for many, there may be some persuading to do!) estate planning, business planning and active asset management, reflecting the transition from flight capital to financial planning.

The competitive environment is notable for the dominance of the US providers, the absence of truly competitive domestic providers and the enduring presence of the Swiss. The herd instinct prevails with regard to strategies. Perhaps for the non-USA providers, given the geographic distance, lack of Latin American corporate heritage and recent instability, it is difficult to throw caution to the wind and become more fully committed to the market with greater onshore presence.

Citibank and Merrill Lynch are remarkable for their physical presence in the market and are clearly anticipating the benefit of being able to provide an extensive range of advisory services, with the added advantage of onshore servicing. In any case, with their extensive operations elsewhere, they can offer the best of both onshore and offshore worlds.

The regulatory and legislative environment continues to change but possibly still not fast enough in some areas. The reforms are wide-ranging and their impact on international private banking concerns taxation, movement of capital, capital market products and the lack of local competition.

Notes

1 *World Wealth Report 1997*, Gemini Consulting and Merrill Lynch International Private Bank.

2 Ingo Walter, *Secret Money*, p. 59.

3 'Uruguay, the Switzerland of South America?', *Euromoney*, 20 June 1996, p. 16.

4 'The Empire is cashing in', *Asia Inc.*, July 1996, p. 24. It is also understood that the tycoon Li Ka Shing moved his $2.8 billion of personal shares in Cheung Kong (Holdings) Ltd to the Cayman Islands to avoid inheritance tax. 'Panama seeking to erase image as dirty money haven', Reuters News Service, 4 March 1996, Union Bank of Switzerland Annual Report 1994.

5 Citicorp Annual Report 1995, Citibank was the only US or European bank to remain in Venezuela under restrictions imposed in the 1970s, and is now operating as a fully fledged local bank. 'Venezuela: Foreign banks face economic reform, regulations', *Economist Intelligence Unit*, 25 June 1996; 'Growth Options', *The Economist*, 14 December 1996, p. 112; 'Latin America: Private bankers repackage services to meet needs of wealthy clients', *Latin Finance*, July 1996, p. 36; 'Bull on the rampage', *Private Banker International*, May 1996.

6 *Business Latin America*, 25 June 1996.

7 'Mexico's great Salinas soap', *The Economist*, 7 December 1996, p. 69. A Convention against Corruption was organised in early 1996 by the organization of American States (OAS). Remarks made at the Council of the Americas Annual Conference, 7 May 1996, reported by *Washington Transcript Service*, 5 June 1996.

CHAPTER SIX

The Middle East

Introduction

The Middle East is a region where uncertainty appears set for the foreseeable future. It is characterised by extreme unevenness of wealth distribution yet is hugely endowed with natural resources that have helped transform the region in the last twenty years. Unquestionably, oil and gas have played a pivotal role in the development of the Middle East. Wealth either state or private has been derived almost entirely from oil and other natural resources, and also from land and property. The region's non-oil exports are tiny even though some countries have successfully diversified their economies. The oil boom reached a peak in the 1970s and early 1980s creating million and billion-petro-dollar fortunes. But the belief often expressed today is that the days of fortune creation on that scale are largely over.

The financial services infrastructure has been able to develop significantly only in times of stability. Beirut is a shadow of its former self. Dubai is challenging Bahrain which took over from Beirut as the leading financial centre in the Middle East. Financial services developments are taking place now that there is a move towards some liberalisation in financial markets. However, needless to say, non-Arab institutions dominate the international private banking scene.

The Middle East is still very much an outward referral region where the demand remains high for confidentiality and for the ability of the organisation to preserve client assets. However, as in other markets, demand has been changing in nature as sophistication levels rise. In response, products and services have been changing to better meet the needs of the more enlightened international investor.

Like some of the region's trade policies, the financial services regulations are protectionist in some markets, preventing foreign institutions from operating in a number of sectors, limiting them to representative offices or excluding them from owning 100% of a Saudi company, for example. Liberalisation is expected to proceed but not necessarily in the same way as in Asia and Latin America, although Saudi Arabia will probably become a full member of the World Trade Organization (WTO).

Wealth and the wealthy

High net worth individual assets originating from the Middle East region was estimated at $1.1 trillion in 1996, about 7% of total high net worth individual assets worldwide.[1] As in Latin America and Africa, wealth in the Middle East is particularly unevenly distributed, with income per capita ranging from about $18 000 in some Gulf sheikhdoms to $280 in Yemen.[2]

Markets

The Middle East represents a diversity of wealth from rich countries to poor relations. Oil and gas revenues in the Gulf states and Saudi Arabia usually belong to the ruler who distributes them generally on the basis of a long-established tribal system, often to an extensive ruling family

- **Saudi Arabia:** This remains one of the major international private banking markets. Wealth is in the hands of the ruling royal family and the social stratum immediately below it typically diplomats and the families that own the top 1000 Saudi companies. The traditional economy was built around the *Hajj*, the annual pilgrimage of the Muslim faith, together with some coastal trade on the Red Sea and the Gulf. Companies were organised in patterns that reflected prominent trading families and some were well positioned when the oil money arrived. Within the Kingdom, there are a number of markets segmented on the basis of geography, and each with its distinctive heritage: Riyadh, a highly cosmopolitan trading centre with immigrants from Syria, Lebanon, Turkey, Palestine and Egypt; Jeddah, which includes Jeddah itself, Mecca and Medina; and the Eastern Provinces which includes Dhahran. Private bankers maintain that these areas have a very distinctive make up particularly across risk and sophistication levels, demanding tailored approaches to introductions and services provided.

- **The United Arab Emirates (UAE):** With a population of 2 million, spread over 7 states, the UAE has the twelfth-highest per capita income worldwide. It is increasingly seen as a critical strategic bridgehead to the markets of the Middle East and the Indian sub-continent, given its position astride major shipping and air routes. The UAE has to some extent reduced its dependency on oil and diversified into agriculture and horticulture.

- **Oman:** Oman is considered one of the more politically stable countries in the region, with a population of only 2 million and private net assets estimated at $2.5 billion, excluding those of the Omani royal family and Diwan, the royal court. Most of the wealthy live in Muscat or in Salalah in the south and are entrepreneurs involved in trade or oil.[3]

- **Kuwait:** A small but hugely wealthy country, thanks largely to oil. In 1996 Kuwait had the fourth-largest oil export revenues in the world. With a population of approximately 2 million, its very high GDP per capita makes it a prime international private banking opportunity, although the number of individuals concerned will be relatively small. Land and property prices have contributed to wealth generation since the end of the Gulf War.

- **Qatar:** Another small country, with a population of 0.6 million, whose economy has been built entirely on gas and oil revenues. The new Amir, who came to power in 1995, having deposed his father, is trying to establish a legal distinction between his father's purse and that of the state, given that the country is in desperate need of capital to fund further investment. Funds in France and Switzerland are currently frozen. Significant wealth is expected in the future from current gas projects that should be exporting gas in 1999.

- **Egypt:** Egypt has been experiencing rising economic growth since 1993, with a steady year-on-year improvement in real GDP growth. The government is committed to a programme of privatisation of state-owned companies. Egypt is seen as an important and expanding private banking marker.

Other smaller markets include the Lebanon, Jordan and Israel.

Drivers of cross-border wealth

The arrival of cross-border wealth from the Middle East is a relatively new phenomenon in the history of international private banking, given that private wealth started to emerge significantly only in the 1970s. The rate and scale of it has been unprecedented. However, these oil-based fortunes have been created in times of profound instability in which the drivers have been:

- **Safety and protection of assets** from changes in social and political fortunes of the wealthy that might result from the overthrow of ruling families and family members or of governments.
- **Diversification of political risk** away from the Middle East where wars in some cases have been a frequent occurrence, and peace has proved elusive.
- **International investment expertise**, given that local markets do not necessarily offer the same range of services and banking sectors are generally weaker than in the more established European and North American financial centres.
- **Supporting international lifestyles**, involving regular travel and the foreign education of children which has meant the establishment of residence and commercial interests abroad.

The drivers of the past differ little from drivers of cross-border wealth today. Europe and the USA are home to many displaced wealthy (or once wealthy) individuals and to displaced wealth. The displaced wealthy includes:

- Iraqis who have sought asylum from Saddam Hussein's regime.
- Iranians, who went into exile after the revolution in 1979, because they were members of the ex-Shah of Persia's family, or had royal connections, or because they were members of the professional classes. An estimated million left the country (and much of their wealth), seeking safety in the USA and elsewhere.

- Wealthy Lebanese who had historical links with France in particular; they re-established themselves and rehoused their wealth during the lengthy civil war.
- Israeli wealth, Jewish wealth, which remains safe from the continuing consequences of the lack of a peace settlement and is geographically widespread, because of the pattern of immigration into Israel.

The commonly held view is that the majority of private wealth is already out of countries such as Iraq, Iran and the Lebanon.

Wealth dynamics

As in all international private banking regions, dynamics relating to wealth creation in the Middle East are noticeably changing. Governments recognise the need to attract private capital held offshore, given the liquidity problems at home. As in other regions, the inheritance factor is beginning to bite and the distribution of wealth is taking place. Women are becoming more visible entrepreneurs - obviously more visible in some countries than in others; and the management of wealth according to Islamic principles is not just a passing fad but is now a well-established banking sector, and not just in the Middle East.

Perhaps Saudi Arabia is one of the better exponents of the creation of wealth through businesses diversification. Fortunes were built on the back of a strong trading heritage and the more recent oil boom, but companies have subsequently diversified into construction, medical and municipal services. Capital for expansion has come from within the organisation resulting in conglomerates with diverse and sometimes disjointed activities and interests. These firms tend to be overcapitalised and underleveraged, or at least in need of rationalisation to achieve greater synergies. However, a growing number of owners want to change the shape of their holdings simply to meet family needs or personal objectives.[4]

Repatriation of wealth

As in Latin America, Middle Eastern wealth flows onshore and offshore, as local economies become more liberal. Key areas of change are the development of the financial markets, privatisation of state-owned industries and utilities, and other investment programmes. A number of the countries, such as Saudi Arabia, have had to look to the private sector rather than the government for funding. Given the focus on capital projects and infrastructure development, there is a belief in some international private banking quarters that repatriated wealth to the Middle East is largely money committed to business diversification, rather than monies looking for alternative forms of investment.

A number of markets are experiencing an inflow of private wealth:

- **Lebanon:** The Prime Minister, Rafik Hariri, is spearheading economic development. Capital inflows have increased; a reported $6.5 billion flowed into the country in 1994, almost double the 1992 level.
- **Oman:** The Sultan has personally intervened and requested that assets previously held abroad be repatriated to help finance infrastructure and industrial projects.
- **Egypt:** Government promises of extensive privatisation have yet to materialise. The government committed itself to selling about $1.5 billion-worth of state assets by the end of 1996; only a small fraction of the 300 or so state-owned firms worth an estimated $25 billion. Private bankers have also reported property as an attractive investment where profits realised have been taken back out of the country.
- **Saudi Arabia:** The two main sources that funded past economic expansion have been the government and banks. The private sector is also regarded as a source of funding. It has been estimated that $125 billion of private-sector wealth is kept offshore.[5] Repatriation was a characteristic of the early 1990s, when more private capital was invested in new ventures from 1991 to 1993 than in the previous ten years. However, momentum was lost because of the Gulf War.

Wealth in the hands of women

International private bankers are beginning to remark on the inheritance factor, particularly in relation to women. With the shift of wealth beginning to take place, on the death of the first generation of wealth creator, undoubtedly there are now growing levels of wealth in the hands of women. Under Islamic law, daughters as well as sons inherit, albeit unequally – on the basis of one part to two parts, in the sons' favour. Where cross-border wealth is concerned, the beneficial owner dictates how the wealth is distributed and some international private bankers detect that a more even-handed approach is now being taken with regard to the sexes. Where the views differ is over how much control and influence these women have over their financial affairs, and over their degree of sophistication and desire to take action. There is a growing level of competitive activity, suggesting that there are enough women to present a sustained marketing opportunity. An indication of this is the increased presence of female private bankers in the region, particularly in the Gulf and Saudi Arabia, where women in business are a new phenomenon.

Islamic wealth[5]

It would not be unreasonable if international private bankers were to covet the funds held in Islamic institutions. Growth rates, ironically, are curtailed by the very people who demand that Islamic money be managed according to the Islamic faith: there is a lack of international consensus on how Islamic banks should be regulated and how monies should be managed. According to unofficial estimates, the worldwide pool of funds being managed according to Islamic principles totals around $100 billion. Wealth that demands Islamic banking services is clearly a growing market. It is recognised, though, as being still on the fringes of international private banking. For many international private bankers, the provision of Islamic services is not on the agenda. However, they are clearly of the view, given their experience, that their clients are looking for non-Islamic ways of wealth management. While there may be an element of incredulity that vast amounts of wealth is deposited without earning interest, the strengthening of the Islamic faith, helped by government backing, will guarantee the growth of Islamic banking, and leading providers of financial services such as Citibank recognise it as a global phenomenon and have responded accordingly.

Needs of the wealthy

International private bankers appear entirely consistent in their belief that there are a number of common denominators across the needs of the various Middle Eastern markets, particularly confidentiality, and confidence in the institution to which the wealth is entrusted, and in the country where the money is invested.

The need for confidentiality is characterised in a number of ways. The importance of Switzerland, particularly Geneva, as a wealth destination for Middle Eastern wealth underlines how high the Middle Eastern wealthy rate confidentiality and anonymity. Servicing the

Middle Eastern wealthy can also be a highly discreet business with certain clients demanding separate entrances in private banking offices or at least to be not left waiting with other clients. Private bankers will say that in their experience this concern over discretion varies and tends to increase with clients from countries where legal constraints are the most restrictive with regard to movement of capital. In any event, Middle Eastern clients believe that the Middle East is a small place and foreign institutions are often better placed to provide discretion and confidentiality than a local institution.

Confidence in the institution is an imperative not least because of collapses in the European banking sector and other financial scandals, including collapse of BCCI. Banking with friends is not the best way of ensuring that personal wealth is protected. In addition, with government ownership of domestic banks being prevalent, as in other countries and regions where the banking sector is weak, there is a fear of appropriation of depositor funds by the government.

The vast changes in the Middle East during the last 25 years have brought growing levels of sophistication, largely as a result of market liberalisation, foreign education and a more international lifestyle. Private bankers still maintain that sophistication levels vary but agree with the general view that investors have become much more shrewd and intent on getting the best deal, in the safe knowledge of the importance of Middle Eastern wealth in the international private banking market.

Financial centres within the Middle East

There are few international financial centres within the Middle East. Given the political unrest within the region, there have been a number of changes to the centres particularly in the last 25 years. Up until the civil war in Lebanon, Beirut was the financial centre of the Middle East, a highly cosmopolitan and international city, often described as the Riviera of the Middle East. The civil war destroyed the city but now it is beginning to recover slowly although still hampered by the lack of peace in the region.

Bahrain[6]

Bahrain has been a beneficiary of both ill fortune and good fortune. It replaced Beirut as the financial centre of the Middle East and benefitted hugely from the oil boom years of the 1970s and early 1980s. The impact of the oil boom was seen largely in the growth of offshore banking units and in the growth of Bahrain's financial sector. Bahrain fortunately remained relatively protected from the effects of the Gulf War.

Foreign banks flooded to the region and set up offshore banking units, hoping to ride the bandwagon of the oil boom and also recognising the absence of domestic competition. At one point these offshore banking units were estimated to hold collectively $67 billion of assets. However, where once there were about 75 offshore banking units in the peak of the mid-1970s, the number has fallen to below 50 (and is expected to continue to fall).

Bahrain has a sophisticated financial infrastructure, it is well located for the Gulf and has a benign regulatory environment. Unlike many neighbouring Gulf countries which allow only limited foreign ownership of companies, Bahrain allows 100% foreign ownership. It is a tax haven and has no foreign exchange controls and no restrictions on repatriation of capital.

International private banking providers often use Bahrain as the base from which to serve other Middle Eastern markets such as the Gulf states and Saudi Arabia. Its geographic position in relation to Saudi Arabia has encouraged a strong link between the two. Bahrain retains a small proportion of wealth within the Middle East region, the rest going to Europe and the USA.

Bahrain now has to compete actively with other local centres such as Abu Dhabi and Dubai, which are growing in sophistication and competing with Bahrain for onshore servicing and the provision of international private banking services.

United Arab Emirates (UAE)

Federation in 1971, the UAE comprises the emirates of Abu Dhabi, Dubai, Sharjah, Ajman, Umm al-Qaiwain, Ras al-Khaimah and Fujairah. It is the first two which are of particular importance to international private banking and which act as local financial centres. Dubai now competes with Bahrain as a financial centre and is in its own right a major trading centre, particularly for Yemen. It offers the tax-free investment zone of Jebel Ali which has recently been provided with significant further investment from the government. Dubai though is not a tax haven like Bahrain. Abu Dhabi has transformed itself from a tiny desert settlement into a thriving, modern city.

Financial centres outside the Middle East

Cross-border wealth from the Middle East typically leaves the region and goes to either Europe or the USA. Europe offers the internationally wealthy from the Middle East a number of choices:

- **Switzerland** provides confidentiality and security and is reputed to have by far the bulk of Middle Eastern private wealth, although the funds are not necessarily held in Switzerland, and fiduciary services are sometimes used.
- **London** is attractive for the inherent security offered by the UK. It also provides access to a wide range of wealth management expertise not found within the Middle East or at least, not wanting to be accessed from within the region. London is used as a centre also in order to avoid political risk. However, the view is expressed sometimes that London is not always attractive to some Middle Eastern clients because of its highly regulated environment and the fear of taxation. Strict residency rules and the possibility of imposition of taxes on offshore investment income are often cited as causes of apprehension in relation to the centre.
- **Channel Islands** as a tax haven provides safety, security and anonymity and competes with Switzerland for funds, particularly with the use of Private Investment Companies (PIC).
- **Luxembourg** appeals to Middle Eastern wealth with Lebanese origins because of its geographic proximity to France. Paris too provides financial services for Lebanese wealth.
- **New York** is the only significant destination outside Europe for wealthy Middle Eastern individuals, attractive for performance and international investment capability and where for lifestyle reasons, like London, wealth needs to be available.

Competitive environment

The competitive environment is dominated by foreign institutions, almost exclusively European and US in origin. Europe is often the launch pad into the Middle East allowing certain product providers relative proximity for marketing and servicing purposes. However, a number of Middle Eastern financial institutions are beginning to gear

Table 6.1 Notable international private banking providers in the Middle East

US banks	Chase Manhattan Bank, Citibank
US investment banks	JP Morgan, Merrill Lynch
European commercial banks	HSBC including British Bank of the Middle East, Coutts, ABN Amro, ING, Lloyds Bank
European merchant banks	Banque Indosuez, Schroders, Fleming, Banque Nationale de Paris, Dresdner Bank (formerly Kleinwort Benson)
European asset managers	Mercury Asset Management and fund management subsidiaries of merchant banks
Middle Eastern banks	Islamic institutions; local banks with growing international capability e.g. Saudi American Bank (SAMBA); Arab Banking Corporation; National Bank of Bahrain; United Bank of Kuwait

up their services to cater for international clients, recognising that foreign institutions have been leading the way and local institutions have been lagging. Whereas foreign institutions in the past have had, on the whole, greater financial know-how, local institutions have the all-important local knowledge and contacts with the wealthy. Middle Eastern institutions typically set themselves up in Switzerland and London.

In addition, there are a number of niche providers catering for the Middle Eastern international private banking client:

- Investcorp, belonging to a privately owned Arab merchant bank focusing on luxury goods businesses worldwide. Investcorp offers private placements.
- Specialist investment companies that assist wealthy individuals in diversifying their business interests worldwide.
- Indicative of the scale of some Middle Eastern wealth for example from Yemen, Lebanon and Saudi Arabia, family offices, though few in number, are well established. They are typically found where a certain level and complexity of wealth would necessitate employing a full-time individual agent or a team to manage the family's offshore wealth and in some cases, their business interests and investments. It is believed that many of the major wealthy families from the Middle East have some form of representation in Europe. A high degree of trust is important in the family office approach, particularly where responsibility for offshore assets takes place away from the region and decisions are taken on behalf of the client.

US providers benefit from the universal appeal of the US origins. European banks, with their geographic proximity, lack of strong local competition and their historical links with the region, are a diverse population of providers and nationalities. For asset managers, the Middle East is attractive for a number of reasons, largely for the big-ticket subscriptions into their funds and the lack of strong local competition to date. Local institutions that are able to make competitive inroads into private wealth are either run on Islamic lines, large enough to have an international network particularly operating in jurisdictions such as London and Switzerland (rarely) or else are highly specialised such as Investcorp.

In some ways, competition has been regulated by protectionist policies such as those that exist in, for example, Saudi Arabia. The financial services sector in that country is protected from foreign competition, in that foreign banks are restricted to having affiliates, such as: Citibank with Saudi American Bank; Banque Indosuez with Al-Bank Al-Saudi Al-Fransi; Hongkong Shangai Banking Corporation (HSBC) with Saudi British Bank; ABN Amro Bank with Saudi Hollandi Bank.

As in other regions, long banking association with the Middle East region has given some providers a head start in the international private banking marketplace. Longevity, the establishment of deep servicing roots, and affinity and association with the market have assisted some of the larger and more international operators to enter the international private banking marketplace. While originally establishing its private banking business in Switzerland, Citibank started to build up London as an alternative centre for the Middle East in the mid-1980s. As well as having New York to add to the servicing conduits for its cross-border business, Citibank has undoubtedly the added advantage of one of the best-recognised names in financial services in the Middle East backed up by physical presence and long-standing businesses in the region. It has been 40 years in both Egypt and Saudi Arabia, 25 in Bahrain and 20 in Oman.[7]

Islamic banking

The Islamic banking sector is still in its infancy and views within the international private banking industry differ as to the nature of its opportunity as far as the Middle Eastern wealthy are concerned. Some will say that clients to date are looking for wealth management along Western lines while others recognise that foreign institutions could have a much greater part to play in managing significant pools of wealth already within Islamic institutions.

Some of the barriers to realising the opportunity are the lack of a money market acceptable under Islamic principles, and of standardised accounting rules. However, notwithstanding the absence of these fundamental components, Islamic banking is a growth sector populated by an estimated 100 institutions, both Islamic and foreign. In some markets, there are dual types of banking services such as exist in Malaysia.

Key elements of Islamic banking are that interest cannot be received and it is prohibited to finance activities banned by the Koran such as alcohol, smoking and gambling. To satisfy religious scholars, a number of tailored product and service alternatives have evolved:[8]

- *Morabaha:* A bank buys a commodity or a piece of equipment on behalf of a customer, then sells it to the customer with a profit margin on a cash or deferred payment basis.
- *Modaraba:* A managing trustee invests funds on behalf of someone else and takes a specified percentage of any profits on the investment.
- *Mosharaka:* A joint-venture agreement in which a bank joins a customer in taking an equity stake in a project. The two parties share the profits or losses in direct proportion to their investments after payment of any agreed management fee.
- *Ijara:* A bank finances the purchase of equipment, buildings and other facilities on behalf of a client, then leases them to him at an agreed rental rate.
- *Ijara-wa-iktina:* A leasing agreement that gives the client a right to buy items once accrued payments have reached a level equal to an agreed sale price.
- *Istisnaa':* A bank finances the production of specified equipment or products with input provided by the customer at an agreed price.

Top Islamic institutions are found throughout the Middle East and Pakistan. The four largest in terms of assets are Al-Rajhi Banking and Investment Corporation (Saudi Arabia), Islamic Development Bank (Saudi Arabia), Kuwait Finance House and Muslim Commercial Bank (Pakistan). Foreign providers that have entered into the provision of Islamic products and services are notably the merchant banks with Islamic funds and they include European providers such as Flemings, Schroders, Kleinwort Benson and Banque Nationale de Paris (BNP).

Furthermore, banks such as ABN Amro and Citibank have established dedicated Islamic banking units in Bahrain. Citibank Islamic Investment Bank has started to roll out a dedicated range of products for high net worth individuals who are seeking to manage their wealth according to Islamic laws. The Citibank products are available worldwide, because the opportunity is recognised as being not only within the Middle East.

Strategies

Referrals are highly dependent on links with senior businessmen, the ruling family or with the next highest social strata. Personal introductions are the key and wooing is often conducted on a social footing. Relationships are key.

For the larger providers, marketing of the region comes typically within the span of European operations and the dual centres of Switzerland and London as well as Bahrain and Dubai. This highlights some of the operating peculiarities of certain organisational structures; for example, each centre marketing the virtues of its own jurisdiction, sometimes aware of each other's movements and at other times, allegedly not.

As in other regions, a number of providers have committed themselves to a growing onshore presence, recognising that the advisory nature of some of their services could be better supported and marketed with constant onshore presence. In the Middle East, this tends to be more a people-driven presence than a physical presence. For some providers, like Citibank and Merrill Lynch, onshore servicing is a consistent strategy worldwide. For others, such as the Swiss and Coutts, changes are not expected; they consider offshore presence to be more appropriate, with regular regional visits to maintain relationships. Certainly, onshore presence can only be on a fairly limited basis given the regulations in place in some markets. Representatives are typically found in Beirut, Dubai, Abu Dhabi, Amman and Saudi Arabia.

Recruitment of staff within Saudi Arabia needs to be in keeping with the government's top priority policy of creating jobs for Saudi citizens – 'Saudisation'. For some international private banking providers, this is not a route they would choose. In others, such as Saudi British Bank, the majority of private banking staff are Saudis.

With such a high degree of confidentiality required, the core proposition of discretionary portfolio management is still a mainstay for cross-border wealth. However, recent developments have reinforced the growing breadth of product demand and sophistication of the Middle Eastern wealthy. The proposition has evolved from cash deposits and portfolio management to include packaged investments and guaranteed derivatives. Of particular significance are:

- Anglo-Saxon trusts, particularly within the jurisdictions of the Channel Islands, which can be favoured vehicles, with the growing use of Private Investment Companies (PICS) providing competition to the anonymity and protection from Switzerland.
- Local brokerage services with onshore servicing in support.
- Specialist products such as derivatives, private placements and private funds.
- Supporting of entrepreneurs and their businesses particularly with corporate services and financing.
- Islamic products and services.
- Commercial and residential property is a distinctive investment preference of Middle Eastern investors. Property investments are typically in London as well as some investment by wealthy Saudis being noted in Lebanon, as the economic recovery begins.
- Estate planning services, particularly for tax avoidance purposes.

Servicing strategies also relate to the type of wealth targeted. For wealth destined for wealth protection, there is little requirement for an onshore presence. For the majority of providers, offshore servicing appears to be the norm, partly because travel with the region is not easy given its size and infrastructure, and because access can be well provided from Europe.

The growth of women private bankers actively pursuing wealth held by Middle Eastern women began in earnest after the Gulf War. In the more liberal environment of the Gulf states, gaining access to wealthy women is not so much of a problem. However, in Saudi Arabia, the operating environment has been considered too prohibitive for some providers to contemplate sending in a female private banker, for once in the Kingdom, the normal codes of conduct prevail such as compulsory chaperoning and segregation. However, some prominent providers, particularly from London, such as Crédit Suisse, Coutts, HSBC and Merrill Lynch, are all actively pursuing wealth in the hands of Middle Eastern women throughout the Gulf and Saudi Arabia and note the success of the strategy of using female private bankers.

Regulatory and legislative environment

In a number of Middle Eastern countries, foreign exchange regulations are still in place.

In contrast to the situation in other regions, privatisation has yet to take off in a significant way. Although there is a great need for privatisation, it is believed that oil money and state spending will continue to prop up development projects. It is uncertain whether governments, for example, those within the Gulf Co-operation Council (GCC), will go as far as to sell their shares in public institutions outright. The more likely scenario is for the private sector to take part in capital projects in the oil, power and water sectors to meet increasing demand from a growing population.

In most Gulf states, foreign firms are limited to 49% ownership of companies, unless in one of the few free-trade zones.

Capital markets remain relatively under-developed. Foreign investment is also limited in Gulf equity markets, where some 300 shares are listed and turnover is estimated at one-fifth of Singapore's.

In Saudi Arabia, for example, progress in assisting economic development is considered slow. Plans for privatising state enterprises, increasing foreign access to Saudi Arabian equity markets and reducing government subsidies are likely to remain on the drawing board. Significant progress is likely only if King Fahd takes a more active role. However, the rise in oil prices is reducing the urgency of implementing economic reforms.

Conclusions and outlook

With political uncertainty characterising the region, the Middle East continues to be an outward referral opportunity. However, a number of international private banking providers are recognising the existence of a different and growing market for more active advisory services onshore, and they are building up their presence in certain centres such as those in the Gulf.

Wealth creation has been largely on the back of the exploitation of natural resources, particularly oil and gas and their spin-offs, together with large rises in land and property prices. Wealth is highly concentrated and is predominantly in the hands of families where family-owned businesses also act as agents for a wide cross-section of business activities too, thereby controlling huge shares of the market. However, notwithstanding the abundance of natural resources, the scale of fortune creation over the past twenty years is not expected to be repeated.

Bahrain and Dubai are the key financial centres, and the usual base in the Middle East for international private banking providers to cover the region, as well as India and Pakistan in some cases. Dubai is now providing stiff competition to Bahrain, the latter being regarded by many as an expensive centre from which to operate. However, international financial centres such as London, Geneva and New York play a major part in servicing and managing wealth sourced from the Middle East and international private bankers from these centres continue to come to the Middle East.

Indicative of the growing sophistication of the financial services sector, Middle East institutions are beginning to address the international private banking opportunity too, but are some way behind the dominant US and European providers, which are the principal providers of international private banking services. Some Middle East institutions have set themselves up in London and Switzerland and they rely for referrals on their network of connections in the Middle East. On the other hand, Middle East institutions will continue to lead the expansion of the Islamic banking sector. Few of the international private banking providers to date have fully addressed this market segment with an appropriate product portfolio. Islamic wealth cannot be ignored, but views differ among international private banking providers as to the extent of demand for these services from their clients.

The main service requirements for clients originating from the Middle East are confidentiality, confidence in the financial institution and confidence in the country where the wealth is invested. Products and services have evolved from the traditional passive proposition of cash deposits and portfolio management. The Middle Eastern client typically has become a much more shrewd and sophisticated investor and, in response, providers have built up a much more developed product proposition to include trusts, derivatives and a range of equity products with a firm emphasis on performance. However, financial sophistication is not universally found in all clients.

The key markets in the Middle East continue to be Saudi Arabia and the Gulf states which, though they have small populations, are hugely wealthy.

As in other regions, a number of wealth dynamics are evident. Repatriation is a characteristic of wealth, but it is not clear how much repatriated wealth is available for investment and how much is reserved for committed business interests. Other wealth trends are the passing-on of wealth from one generation to another with the death of the founding father. Significantly, and in contrast to other regions, a discreet marketing opportunity has arisen in connection with female inheritors.

Notes

1 *World Wealth Report 1997*, Gemini Consulting and Merrill Lynch.
2 'Integration? You must be joking', *The Economist*, 16 November 1996, p. 79.
3 *Global Private Banking*, 13 November 1995.
4 *Middle East Economic Digest*, August 1995.
5 'Prophet Sharing', *Wall Street Journal (Europe)*, 15 February 1996, p. 1.
6 Bahrain Monetary Agency, as reported in *Global Private Banking*, 1 April 1996; *Middle East Economic Digest*, 18 December 1995, p. 41; *Wall Street Journal*, 15 February 1996.
7 Citicorp Annual Report 1995.
8 'Looking good on papyrus', *The Economist*, 24 August 1996, p. 73; Islamic Investment Company of the Gulf.
9 'Gulf states' privatisation move making slow progress', *New Straits Times*, 4 February 1997; Saudi Arabia Country Report, No. 1, 1997, *Economist Intelligence Unit*.

CHAPTER SEVEN

Domestic private banking – a worldwide perspective

Introduction

Like its international counterpart, domestic private banking is fast becoming one of the most important developments in financial services worldwide. Providers in all the regions now recognise the opportunity presented by greater wealth creation and distribution. However, developments are at different stages and only some markets are showing significant advances. More evolved markets such as the USA and UK are where the changes are much more evident.

The major dynamics within the domestic private banking arena worldwide are:

- The growing wealth pools of wealth held domestically, estimated at three times the level of wealth held internationally.
- The different stages at which financial services providers are recognising the opportunity to serve their more wealthy clients.
- The cross-section of competitor types taking advantage of deregulation and the market opportunity.

However, notwithstanding the structural alterations already under way in the industry, domestic private banking is still largely in its infancy worldwide.

The major competitor type found in all domestic private banking markets is the retail bank. Typically, though, banks face a challenge from non-banks. The strength of competition coming from the non-bank population varies from one market to another but in those that are more sophisticated, non-banks are a constant presence and, for some bank providers such as those in the USA, a constant pressure. Helped along by deregulation, non-banks are undoubtedly providing healthy competition where private banking is no longer the exclusive domain of banks.

Industry evolution of domestic private banking

It could be said that the development of domestic private banking represents a rebirth for banks. Traditionally, banks always focused on wealthy individuals. It is only more recently in the 1970s and 1980s in Western markets such as in Europe and North America that banks moved away from their traditional market and entered mass market retail banking. It is now in the 1990s that banks have come full circle and are refocusing on the wealthy. The difference now is that banks have a bulk of mass-market customers to serve profitably, together with a much larger customer base of wealthy individuals with more complex needs than hitherto.

Market forces

Market forces supporting the industry evolution closely resemble those that drive international private banking. The development of the domestic private banking industry depends not only on having the raw material of investible wealth but also on a number of key criteria being met. These include a financial services infrastructure that can meet the needs of the market, and a political and economic outlook that is attractive enough to eliminate the need to place monies cross-border.

- **Scale and nature of personal wealth:** Some of the biggest changes in personal wealth creation and distribution are the result of savings, rising incomes and often increased levels of disposable income; rising estate values often inflated by property values and stock market values; and a growing number of business start-ups, flotations and sales. Governments have also been instrumental in wealth creation in the domestic market using a range of incentives and tools such as tax-efficient investment products, new products such as personal pension plans, and mandatory savings plans. Sources of wealth now differ significantly from the past. New wealth is characterised by wealth generated through business - largely sales of businesses, inheritance on different scales where property and business play an important part, and through the high earnings of professionals and executives.

- **Demographics and growing number of wealthy individuals:** In the past, wealth was typically in the hands of families, mainly the landed classes, aristocracy and royalty, and passed down through the generations. Wealth was in the form of property, land and, more recently, stocks and shares. The domestic wealth markets today are characterised by wealth in the hands of a much broader range of socio-economic groupings, often representing the middle market and the middle classes. Key socio-economic groups are retired people, professionals and entrepreneurs together with segments that are created by life-stage events such as inheritances. This type of wealth growth and the change in demographics have been termed the 'beta bulge', to describe the distribution of wealth over a broader cross section of socio-economic groups. Age is an important defining criterion and relates to inheritance and the reaching of a different life stage, such as retirement. Of particular significance are the 'baby boomers', children born soon after the Second World War, now moving from the borrowing stage and becoming savers and investors as well as inheritors of wealth, together with the elderly.

- **Change in demand:** As on the international side, a number of behaviour and attitude changes are detected as a new generation of wealth holders emerges. Key changes are identified within usage of financial services, needs, sophistication levels, and propensity to take action towards wealth management, and attitude to risk and to providers. With rising awareness of financial services and generally higher levels of sophistication, behaviour today is typically more demanding and segmented than in the past. Needs often relate initially to single-product solutions and in more advanced markets they can develop to a broader more integrated wealth management requirement.

- **Political outlook:** Stability and the nature of governments contribute to the decision to retain assets onshore. Less turbulent changes and fewer swings of government are contributing to the development of domestic private banking, as is the move towards democratic, capitalist-oriented governments. Stability within the domestic political scene is key to retention of wealth onshore; in Latin America the change in political outlook and the growing levels of repatriated funds are encouraging the budding domestic private banking industry in that region.
- **Economic outlook:** Strong domestic economic growth has been one of the key motives for the retention onshore of personal wealth and investment, eliminating the need to go offshore. The USA is a classic onshore market where strong economic growth with enduring political stability has precluded the development of a significant offshore market in the traditional sense.
- **Regulation and legislation:** Coupled with the need for a stable political outlook is the requirement for a developed financial services industry to satisfy the needs of the wealthy. The development of stock markets and diversity of investment instruments are other factors favouring domestic private banking, eliminating the need to go offshore and to other international centres to find the necessary product and service options. In addition, fiscal policy and wealth taxes both have a bearing on movement of wealth.

Rationale for entry into domestic private banking

Clearly, rising levels of wealth creation have prompted banks to refocus on domestic private banking. Other reasons, though, stem from less opportunistic reasons. In the 1980s, changing profit dynamics, lending problems both at home and abroad intensified the focus, particularly within the bank population, on low-capital, fee-earning business lines such as private banking. Change in focus has been competitor driven, for example in the USA where deregulation and the cost of deposits were also altering the traditional sources of revenue. So much so, that banks had to start changing their portfolio structure and increasing their non-interest income.

Although banks will maintain that their corporate goal is to increase market share, acquiring new clients from other banks is not a primary motive for entering the domestic private banking market. For retail banks, in the UK for example, the rationale has been defensive in nature. They have seen their affluent customers, often their more profitable customers, courted by other providers and a number depart. With highly prized customers walking out of the door, banks have been spurred into action to protect their high net worth clients. This is often seen as more of a priority than going on the offensive and gaining market share.

For most non-banks, the objective has been precisely to capture market share. Their ethos has been one of hunting rather than farming. In the USA, brokerage houses and mutual fund providers, as groundbreakers in new products and services, have attracted deposits away from banks into a more sophisticated and extensive range of products. This non-bank population has made a virtue out of not having a physical delivery network and has brought innovation and marketing expertise to the affluent marketplace.

Comparison with international private banking

While there are a number of general trends that closely resemble those in international private banking, there are also some key differences:

- Providers of domestic private banking services target both the wealthy and the more modestly wealthy; the profile of both may be relatively simple where domestic sources of wealth are concerned. Client assets are treated as resident and domiciled for tax purposes.
- Needs are often simpler than having to address worldwide sources of income and assets. Client objectives in more sophisticated domestic markets will relate largely to financial planning and importantly to local tax efficiency, with regard to personal income taxes as well as capital and other wealth taxes such as estate duties and inheritance tax.
- Products address a full range of life-stage requirements including money transmission, lending, investments, and protection, pensions, tax and estate planning. The products are designed with local tax regulations in mind; some can be used as tax-planning tools.
- Given that assets are held onshore, risk diversification of assets is largely for investment purposes rather than diversification away from extreme political and economic risk, although the latter has a bearing on investment diversification.

- Domestic private banking clients are provided with a dedicated onshore private banker, often located close to the client and one who can be active and visible within the client's social and professional community.
- The requirement for banking confidentiality between provider and client still stands. However, the desire on the part of the client will be more for discretion than cast-iron secrecy.

Evolution of domestic private banking worldwide

Domestic private banking is at varying stages of evolution around the world. The regions and the markets can be categorised according to their different evolutionary stages, using the following criteria:

- Scale of personal wealth creation and market sizing.
- Sophistication of market and needs.
- Diversity of competition.
- Development of domestic financial services infrastructure.

Key stages so far in the evolution of the domestic private banking industry can be identified as follows:

Embryonic: where there is early recognition of the opportunity; some changes made in services; evolving financial markets; possible vestiges of economic and political instability; product approach to wealth management; highly concentrated wealth.

Evolving: where there is rapid growth of competitor activity; deregulation allowing greater diversity of provider type; little differentiation between strategies; strong growth among providers; greater wealth distribution and segmentation of market.

Transition: where certain providers aggressively acquire market share; providers beginning to differentiate themselves with changes in strategy e.g. alliances; diverse needs of wealthy emerging, driving segmented propositions; initial retreats from market.

Asia[1]

There are predictions that with the long-lasting and rapid economic growth in Asian markets, particularly the rising levels of GDP, and consistently high savings ratios, this could be the biggest domestic private banking market worldwide. Unburdened by commitments to a welfare state like markets in Europe and North America, Asian emerging markets have some of the highest savings rates worldwide in some cases such as East Asia, where the rate reaches 34%. But to date, Asia is largely still an offshore private banking market. The key question is how the market will drive the evolution of a domestic private banking industry and how closely it will resemble North American and European models.

Hong Kong and, recently, Singapore, are the only two examples of evolved domestic private banking markets in the region. In other markets such as Thailand, Indonesia, Malaysia, Taiwan and the Philippines, domestic private banking is at an embryonic stage. Industry evolution is dependent on a number of drivers, namely deregulation, further developments in the capital markets and greater diversity of investment instruments as well as a certain scale of wealth creation and distribution.

Perhaps it is market behaviour that is holding back the more classical development of domestic private banking as found in Europe and North America. Allegedly, high net worth individuals hold significant wealth offshore. Wealth held onshore is typically committed to business, property investments and the domestic stock market if performance is positive. New wealth is closely linked to entrepreneurial activities. Asian countries (apart from Japan) do not have the ageing demographic profile that Western countries have, or the wealth pattern of inheritances.

However, in banks and markets there is keen interest in domestic private banking generally and a recognition that the more wealthy customers need a distinctive and tailored service proposition. In some markets, banks are addressing their higher net worth clients primarily at the banking service level, by putting in place a dedicated manager. Responsibilities of this manager typically focus on execution rather than advice. Compare this with Europe where a domestic private banking division might be staffed by some six hundred people, wholly dedicated to high net worth individuals. Alternatively, broking services for the local stock market is often the central service. High levels of trading activity and a desire for control and decision making are characteristics of many wealthy Asians who invest directly in the local stock market. This can present a market barrier to following the more Western style of private banking that at its more sophisticated stage provides an integrated wealth management approach.

Products offered are typically from the in-house range and include

Table 7.1 Asian stock markets 1996

	Market capitalisation as at October 1996 US$ billion	Number of stocks listed	Daily trading volume US$ million
Japan	3,621	2,287	5,078
Hong Kong	405	560	436
Australia	269	1,186	355
Malaysia	272	576	137
Taiwan	227	364	669
Singapore	181	215	137
South Korea	170	740	206
India	152	5,800	76
Thailand	107	448	49
Indonesia	77	247	36
Philippines	72	212	41
China (B shares)	3	41	3

Source: Morgan Stanley Research.

straightforward banking and deposit products. Some providers address more complex requirements and assist entrepreneurs more directly in wealth creation; this is typical of emerging market economies, where trade finance, corporate finance assistance and lending, either for share transactions, overseas investment or business needs, are provided.

Asian capital markets are still relatively small compared with some of their Western counterparts. Japan remains by far the largest stock market in Asia in terms of market capitalisation, followed by Hong Kong (see Table 7.1).

The regulatory environment can be restrictive, particularly for foreign providers as to the provision of licences to operate as a domestic branch or as a foreign bank branch, the number of branches allowed and products to be offered. True market forces are therefore not so evident in some Asian countries as they are in the more advanced markets. There is evidence of some relaxation on the numbers of foreign banks allowed, for example in the Philippines. However, Malaysia remains restrictive towards foreign banks in terms of distribution and products permitted. Major foreign competitors in Asia remain Standard Chartered with its Priority Banking Service, Citibank and Hongkong Bank. However, in the case of the latter, sizeable wealthy individuals are generally referred to the bank's international private banking service.

Europe[2]

Like other regions, Europe is characterised by a diversity of market stages but the domestic private banking industry is predominantly at the evolved stage. Arguably the UK is the only European market fast approaching transition. Across the markets, large commercial banks have been starting up domestic private banking services since the late 1980s and some much more recently. There tend to be two broad markets, the very wealthy and the middle-tier wealth, which are differently segmented and supported.

A strategy common to many banks has been to set up focused and discreet domestic private banking operations within their retail banking sector, with dedicated relationship managers and support teams. Day-to-day banking services are often still provided through the retail bank. However, most large operators have established large, organisationally separate private banking divisions, depending on their retail bank branches to refer clients to them. In markets such as France, Germany, the Netherlands, Spain, Belgium and Switzerland, foreign competition is making little headway, given the strength of indigenous providers. Where present, foreign providers' are usually highly focused.

In contrast to Asia and the highly active trading levels of its investors, needs in Europe are by no means homogeneous and they vary according to risk appetite. Levels of wealth do not necessarily correlate to sophistication. Strong preferences are still in evidence for low-risk products such as government bonds, for example in the Netherlands and Germany, although this preference is partly related to yield. The appetite for equities is slowly taking off, but only the more sophisticated markets are interested in international equities.

France and Italy illustrate the different stages of the domestic private banking industry; France being at an evolved stage and Italy still in the embryonic stage.

France

High net worth individuals have a long history of services provided by banks, particularly merchant banks and privately owned banks. Today, the major providers are large merchant banks with the traditional reputation of providing services to the wealthy; niche private banking specialists, small privately owned banks and, more recently, retail banks. Providers either focus on the top levels of wealth, typically at least \$1 million of investible assets, or the middle market, typically at least \$100 000 of investible assets.

Investment products and advisory services generally are more developed for the higher wealth levels and include tailored investment management and estate planning services, although banks are beginning to develop a financial planning approach for the middle market. However, the well-developed SICAV industry with high penetration of collective investment schemes of the high net worth sector means that only a small percentage of funds remain under discretionary management.

Italy

Unlike some of the other European domestic private banking markets the dominant providers of private banking services are foreign institutions, both European and US, many of which have long servicing histories in Italy. Local banks provide little competition to the foreign entrants. Local providers are typically deposit and asset management oriented and lack the integrated wealth management proposition more readily available from foreign banks.

Major concentrations of wealth are found in northern Italy. Apart from old money, newer wealth is in the hands of entrepreneurs and professionals.

The selection of a private banking provider depends on a number of reasons; the client is either looking for a better banking service not found in a local bank or wants a more diverse range of products, which again are more readily available from the foreign providers. Investments selected have a history of being conservative and low risk including products such as government securities.

The bureaucratic nature of the regulatory system has been a brake on product development. Furthermore, political instability has made wealthy individuals careful about provider selection and investment products. International private banks have a distinct advantage in being able to diversity wealth globally.

Latin America[3]

Economic and political reforms have aided the emergence of domestic private banking, although the industry is still only embryonic. Classical characteristics of what drives this evolution have been:

- Growing government stability and continuity.
- Economic growth and increased stability.
- Free-market policies encouraging wealth creation.

- Opening up of capital markets and deregulation including privatisation programmes.

Development of services to the wealthy are a consequence of the twin forces of repatriated wealth and new wealth being created. However, repatriation is a function of economic and political stability and domestic investment is still commonly made from offshore. Savings rates are poor compared with Asia's. Exceptionally, Chile with its private pension system has raised its savings rates dramatically from 8.2% of GDP in 1981 to 27.6% in 1995. However, the regional savings rate is 21%.

Key wealth holders are wealthy families, entrepreneurs and professionals. Attitudes to investment products are yield and risk-driven with benchmarks such as domestic interest and inflation rates being of prime consideration. Furthermore, the region's economic history has encouraged a short-term perspective to investment.

Services provided to the wealthy onshore have expanded rapidly as capital markets have developed through deregulation, a prime catalyst being privatisation programmes designed to develop the capital markets and attract foreign investment. In Brazil, the mutual fund industry has been growing rapidly and between 1995 and 1996 it grew 44%, from $67 billion to $100 billion.

Domestic products offered to wealthy Latin Americans range from an extensive range of mutual funds, debt and equity products, particularly fixed-income securities such as Latin American bonds, certificates of deposits and banking services. Sometimes more specialised products such as derivatives are available and, in order to offer international exposure, some local providers have established alliances with international brokers.

Foreign banks, particularly Citibank, have made early inroads into the provision of services to the wealthy in major Latin American markets, taking advantage of weaker banking sectors. A number of US and European providers have a domestic focus, but tend to target the top end of Latin American wealth, typically requiring at least $1 million of investible assets. Most foreign providers, however, are more securely positioned as international providers and will lose out to domestic and local banks particularly if they do not get access to high-yielding domestic products.

Middle East[4]

Domestic private banking services are found in the Gulf States and more so in Saudi Arabia, where domestic private banking is at an embryonic stage.

Saudi Arabia

Domestic private banking has been emerging since the 1980s to address wealth created through the oil boom. However, Saudi institutions dominate the scene as no foreign bank has been allowed to set up a direct presence in the Kingdom since the financial system was Saudi-ised by law in the 1970s. There have not been any new entrants to the banking sector since Al-Rajhi Banking and Investment Corporation was converted into a bank in 1987.

Many of the top ten commercial banks are providing private banking services to their customers, with Saudi American Bank (SAMBA) leading the way. As an affiliate of Citibank, this is perhaps not surprising. Developments have included a Swiss subsidiary and an investment management subsidiary in London, competing with international private banking services. National Commercial Bank (NCB), the largest bank in Saudi Arabia in terms of assets, started in private banking service in 1993. There is little competition beyond the top Saudi banks.

With extreme concentrations of wealth, the market is relatively small in terms of number of individuals compared with size of the total population. Target markets range from the very wealthy, typically having $1.5 million of investible wealth, representing about 12 000–15 000 individuals, to the middle ground of individuals with at least $500 000 of investible assets. As in international private banking, domestic institutions are targeting women, recognising that the death of a husband or father places wealth in the hands of women, in accordance with Islamic inheritance law.

Products included are a full range of banking services together with additional services like corporate banking, corporate finance, investment management, mutual funds and international services through foreign subsidiaries in, for example, Switzerland and London. Presence tends to be confined to Jeddah and Riyadh but NCB has a total of five offices. SAMBA is due to open another office in Al-Khobar, but with its retail branches it is able to provide services in Makkah, Buraidah and Medina amongst other locations. Services provided to men and women are segregated and female relationship officers provide the service to their lady customers.

North America[5]

The USA has the largest domestic private banking market in the world, in terms of current investible levels of assets. It is also one of the more advanced markets and is fast approaching transition as evidenced by a growing divide between the main providers, the development of segmented services and the adoption of strategies to address the diverse needs.

Canada

Like other markets, Canada has introduced significant deregulation in the financial services industry. Key legislative reforms took place in 1987 and 1992, which removed operating barriers for banks where previously they were restricted in what products they could offer. Today, banks can now own trust companies, investment brokerages and insurance companies although they are still prohibited from selling insurance products through their branch network. As in many domestic markets, the competition is fragmented, with the five largest Canadian banks all operating on a relatively equal footing. However, the Royal Bank of Canada stands apart with its international network (28 private banking units in 22 countries).

'Baby boomers' dominate the marketplace and are increasingly savers and buyers of wealth management services. A private banking client would typically have US$500 000 of investible assets.

Integrated wealth management is now well evolved thanks largely to deregulation. Previously, services were lending and credit oriented and typically transactional in nature. Services include banking, investment management, brokerage and estate planning.

Providers today in the domestic private banking market

Domestic providers of services to the wealthy were traditionally the privately owned banks and latterly the private banking departments of the larger incorporated banks, the commercial banks. However, today, there is a diversity of providers reflecting deregulation, relative strengths and weaknesses of providers, differences of evolution within financial services industries and relative strengths of the financial services industries. Providers of services to the wealthy have evolved along the lines described overleaf.

Privately owned family banks

These are a rare breed, not often found today. Certain markets such as Europe and the USA still boast a few but the decrease in number is due largely to the growing strength of the commercial banks which outcompete the privately owned banks and expose the balance sheet, product range and distribution limitations often associated with this type of provider.

- In the USA, Riggs and Brown Brothers Harriman still remain.
- In Germany, the banking sector is characterised by regional privately owned banks, some struggling to survive. Numbers are reducing.
- In the UK, C Hoare and Co is the last remaining family owned, partnership-style bank; Cazenove is a family-owned stockbroker.
- In Asia, in Thailand and the Philippines for example, a number of banks are family owned or at least a family is the majority shareholder.
- In Brazil and Chile, in contrast to the large number of government-owned banks and against a background of banking collapses, there are a number of established and successful banks still privately owned.

Once privately owned, now owned by commercial banks

It is more typical in Europe to find these once privately owned banks now in the hands of the large commercial banks, the latter acquiring an upmarket brand as part of their portfolio for servicing customers, using the brand either to appeal to their existing customers or as a means of attracting new customers. In most cases, the brand name continues to operate under its independent name:

- In Germany, Deutsche Bank owns Bank Grunelius, a Frankfurt-based private bank; HSBC owns Trinkhaus und Burkhardt.
- In Switzerland, there have been a number of acquisitions by the three large commercial banks which have also included small private banks with a domestic and international franchise.

Private banking franchise developed within a commercial bank

Some of the larger banks have built up their domestic private banking franchise from scratch, typically from a base of providing traditional services on a more passive, on-request basis. In Europe and the USA, the extensive franchise existing through the bank relationship gives the retail banking arms of commercial banks a major advantage. Commercial banks with a retail banking arm are a major force in domestic private banking today throughout Europe.

- In Germany, Deutsche Bank and Dresdner Bank are the leading retail banks and, for that matter, domestic private banking providers. The banks have nationwide coverage and scale, with Deutsche Bank utilising its branch network to support its clients on a day-to-day basis, and it also has 260 dedicated asset management centres all over Germany. Commerzbank and Bayerische Vereinsbank, other retail banks, have recently followed.
- ABN dominates the Netherlands. It has regional private banking offices as well as its retail bank branches.
- In Spain, Privanza and Banco Banif are two of the largest domestic private banking providers.

Non-banks

The non-bank threat comes in a variety of forms depending on the industry structure and the level and type of regulations in place. The non-bank population normally consists of fund managers, brokers and insurance companies.

- In the USA, non-banks, in particular the mutual fund providers and full service brokerage houses, are the single most important threat to banks.
- In the UK, non-banks are well established in the domestic private banking marketplace and include fund managers and independent financial advisers. However, the general intensity of competition from this quarter is somewhat less for banks than it is in the USA.
- In the Netherlands, the insurance companies compete with banks in providing services to the wealthy.

- In Asia, brokers are active suppliers of trading services on the domestic markets, often with dedicated units for high net worth individuals.

Professionals

Consistently across the markets, professionals such as lawyers, tax managers and accountants, have had a long-established relationship with wealthy individuals. While some of their expertise has been introduced into the larger banking organisations, generally they remain appreciated and trusted by wealthy individuals; hence the incentives for referrals set up between banks and professionals. In some markets, such as the UK, changes to regulations now allow solicitors to manage investment portfolios. On the whole, though, the professionals have remained within their natural constituencies of law, tax and accounting.

Domestic versus foreign providers

In the more advanced markets with strong banking sectors, domestic private banking providers are the dominant forces in the market. Where foreign institutions are strong, this typically reflects a weaker and more immature domestic financial services infrastructure. Alternatively, where little foreign presence is in place, this is due to either strong domestic competition and/or restrictive policies on foreign bank entry, often found in the embryonic markets of Asia. Citibank is the universal competitor throughout domestic private banking markets.

Developments within the retail banking sector

In a number of markets worldwide, it is developments within the retail banking sector that are creating some of the biggest competitive stirs. In Europe and North America, for example, most of the large commercial banks have entered domestic private banking. However, moving into private banking where hitherto services were unsegmented requires more than rolling out a red carpet, a hackneyed image associated with servicing the wealthy. The changes that have taken place are deep set and include cultural change. For banks, often regarded as being resistant to change, slow moving and risk adverse, this has been quite a challenging test.

The most evident changes are best illustrated in the advanced markets of the USA and UK where many are well under way.

People

Private banking staff, whether relationship managers, technical experts or support staff, generally have a different profile from their retail banking counterparts, reflecting the need to deliver higher service levels, manage relationships over a long period of time and provide technically complex products that can also include products from a range of providers. Importantly, private banking staff are now more often formally recruited. Evidence in both the UK and USA indicates that banks are no longer content to reshuffle the pack of existing staff. Specially designed recruitment programmes to select private banking staff from within existing personnel are more the norm. Recruitment also takes place outside the bank to fill specialist posts or where existing staff cannot fill posts.

The roles and responsibilities of the private banking jobs have been designed to emphasise the distinctive servicing requirements, the support roles which typically are team based, and the back-office operations, many of which in the past have been combined roles or undertaken by completely separate departments.

Products

The domestic private banking products of banks have evolved and developed from different starting points, from lending to trusts, from investments to broking. Very few domestic private banks have retained their traditional product constituents, especially where the strategic aim is to be a full service provider to wealthy individuals. Key developments have been to diversify, particularly towards investments reflecting the core wealth-management opportunity and, for some investment-oriented providers, to introduce a banking proposition. More often than not this is a recruitment tool rather than a core wealth-management tool. A full range of domestic private banking services would typically include the following:

- Banking services which now include multi-currency and money market accounts, enhanced card facilities, and flexible lending particularly for mortgages.
- A range of protection products such as life assurance backed products.

- Asset management services which now include a range of portfolios in which to invest with differing risk profiles, depending on the risk and equity appetite of the investor, on a discretionary and advisory basis. Trusts, broking, tax planning and estate planning, insurance, pensions.
- More specialised products such as access to derivatives, unquoted equities, private placements, international equities and emerging market funds where these are demanded by individuals with higher sophistication levels.
- Segmented services for the emerging affluent where tailored products and services are provided. This is more typical of the USA and includes cash management and wrap accounts.

Product enhancements also reflect the profile of the market and often address the corporate requirements of the client and include corporate finance facilities.

Products and services are often branded 'private banking', to differentiate the service and the products are made available to address increased wealth levels and the tax position.

Although not universally the case in all markets, private banking clients generally will be provided with a choice of products from in-house to third-party products, reflecting the general demand for objective and independent advice as well as organisational appetite to take on the task. Meeting regulatory standards in the arena of investments, in particular, can be significant.

Private banker

The private banker is typically a professionally qualified, experienced, mature individual who can be from any one of a variety of backgrounds including banking, corporate finance, law, tax, accountancy, insurance, general financial services and so on, depending on the type of domestic private banking model and the market profile. Professional qualifications are widely recognised and understood by the market and are an important aspect of credibility as well as technical competence.

The private banker has become a single point of contact who will co-ordinate the technical back-up through a team of product experts as well as provide access to parent-group expertise. However, remuneration policies are only slowly beginning to reflect the importance of the role. Remuneration levels on the domestic private banking side lag behind those in international private banking considerably.

Service

A feature of the typical private banking service is the extensive availability of the private banker outside officer hours as well as flexible ways of making contact - face to face, either at home or in the office or private banking office, or by telephone, fax and on-line computer.

Levels of service are high and one of the key areas of service is proactive provision of advice with formalised reviews of financial affairs. This can also be a compliance requirement. Product reporting is frequent and can be tailored to the needs of the client; for example, investment portfolio reporting can be standardised at quarterly intervals and then be increased to monthly and so on.

Frequency of contact varies, depending on the client, and can be fairly passive from half yearly to even annually - often at the request of the client, to a much higher frequency of monthly and weekly. Such levels of service have a direct bearing on how many clients an individual private banker can cater for. On the whole, the higher the number of clients, the less active the service will be. Number of relationships managed by private bankers will vary but can be as high as 150.

Services can extend beyond the immediate financial arrangements to include assistance with property searches, schools for children and travel arrangements. However, the private banker particularly when part of a retail bank, is often supported by the retail bank branch with day-to-day banking services.

One of the biggest issues for domestic private banks that develop within a retail banking sector is organisational structure. For the retail bank, there is no single blueprint, as evidenced by the different models found among the banks in the UK, for example. However, regardless of the model, private banking within a retail banking structure requires some degree of integration or at the very minimum, co-operation between the two entities. Drivers of structure revolve around cost effectiveness, product expertise, market demands, compliance and regulatory parameters, internal accounting practices and the clear delineation of roles with regard to accountability and responsibility.

Client needs

There are a number of attributes required of a domestic private banking business to be successful in the market. These attributes are important for almost all wealthy individuals and have a strong bearing on products, services and delivery.

- Independent and objective advice.
- Active management and service.
- Investment style.
- Value for money.
- Discretion.
- Continuity of service.
- Trust in the individual and organisation.
- Rapport with the private banker.
- Security of assets.
- Image and style of the provider.

Other factors that also influence market behaviour are risk appetite, particularly appetite for equities; level of control over financial affairs; extent of other professional relationships and source of wealth, for example business related wealth.

Key success factors

Looking at the future, across domestic private banking markets, many of the important issues relate to:

- Providers developing and tailoring a private banking proposition to match the market profile.
- Competition, particularly where markets are at the embryonic and evolving stage.
- Product and service expansion, remuneration, service segmentation and development from the 'one service fits all' approach to address distinctive servicing needs of the various segments.
- Differentiation from other bank and non-bank providers.
- Shortages of skilled individuals.

However, the key success factors relate not only to these current and more topical issues but also to the organisation's ability to address the market opportunity fully and not be constrained or influenced by internal matters.

Key success factors are:

- The provider must be able to gain access to the wealthy, nurture the relationship and retain the relationship over an extended period of time.
- The private banker must be suitably skilled and technically qualified to build a relationship that will be founded essentially on trust.
- Advice and service provided must respond to the client's requirements and as full a range of products as possible must be made available.
- To respond to the market's demand for a range of sophisticated products and high levels of service, there must be technical back-up and operational efficiency.
- The style and image of the provider needs to be appropriate for the market and the future market.

Notes

1 'Second wave', *The Economist*, 22 March 1997, p. 88.

2 'The role of high street banks in popularising private banking in France', *World Banking and Securities*, Volume 6, Number 2, Deloitte Touche Tohmatsu International p. 70, 'The outsiders come in', Italian Survey, *Private Banker International*, May 1995, p. 6.

3 *The Economist*, 23 November 1996; 'Banks readjust as wealth comes home', Country update: Brazil. *Private Banker International*, July/August 1996, p. 10; 'Brazil-wealth atlas', *Global Private Banker*, 5 February 1996, p. 10; Brazilian Securities Commission, 1996.

4 Special report on Saudi banking; *Middle East Economic Digest*, 10 May 1996; 'An exclusive service for millionaires and billionaires - private banking', Special Report, *Saudi Gazette*, 8 January 1996.

5 Top ten commercial banks in Saudi Arabia by total assets (1995) are NCB, Riyadh Bank, Saudi American Bank, Arab National Bank, Al-Rajhi Banking and Investment Corporation, Al-Bank Al-Saudi Al-Fransi, Saudi British Bank, Saudi Cairo Bank, Saudi Hollandi Bank, USCB, Saudi Investment Bank, Bank al-Jazira. Source: *Middle East Economic Digest*.

6 'Private Banking in Canada', *World Banking and Securities*, Volume 6, Number 2, Deloitte Touche Tohmatsu International, p. 6.

CHAPTER EIGHT

UK

Introduction

The UK is part way through a major phase of personal wealth creation, the scale and scope of which is evident in a number of ways. Firstly, personal wealth is growing out of all recognisable historic proportions and secondly, personal wealth is much more widely dispersed than ever before. These twin forces of growth and distribution are fuelling, the creation of a new and large market of wealthy individuals who have swelled the high net worth population. They represent an opportunity for existing providers of private banking services and more importantly, for new providers. But the full force of personal wealth creation is yet to be felt in the UK.

Domestic private banking was once the exclusive domain of a small tightly knit group of advisers. Today, providers include the traditional providers, new providers modelled on the traditional ones, and retail banks, typically aiming for broader appeal in the market. Retail banks, more specifically the clearing banks in the UK, are spearheading the domestic private banking revolution and are potentially the most powerful players in the competitor arena today with a natural link with the market opportunity, given their existing customer franchise. It is not, though, a foregone conclusion that they will automatically reap the harvest of wealth. They will have to earn their right to this harvest.

Distinct from the situation in the USA, wealth creation in the UK is largely a result of inflation of asset values through property and the stock market, savings, inheritance and more recently, earnings through employment including high salaries, bonuses and executive options. A number of forces that are driving the desire for financial advice and the changed set of needs have their roots in key changes in the economic outlook in the UK over the last decade.

Wealth and the wealthy

Until now, wealth in the UK has always been confined to a tiny minority, typically the landed gentry, the aristocracy and families and individuals made wealthy through business or industry. Consequently, wealth has always been strongly linked to inheritance and particular socio-economic classes. Today, though, the size and dynamics of the domestic private banking market bear little resemblance to the past.

It is the creation of a middle tier of wealthy individuals in the UK that is one of the most striking dynamics within personal wealth creation in the UK. It has been estimated that there are just under one million high net worth individuals, defined as those having at least £100 000 of investible assets. This equates to around £160 billion of investible wealth and £400 billion of total wealth. The vast majority of these wealthy individuals, some 80%, are found in the middle tier of wealth having under £200 000 of investible wealth. However, wealth is still concentrated significantly in the upper wealth brackets; two-thirds of investible wealth is in the hands of 20% of high net worth individuals.[1] The market seems to naturally divide into two tiers of personal wealth.

Key segments

The private banking market has evolved beyond what is typically referred to as 'old money' where wealth was inherited through the family and where long associations were established with a small group of professional advisers. The new segments are diverse in age, socio-economic class, financial sophistication, lifestage and lifestyle. The largest segments by far in the domestic banking market are the elderly affluent, retired people and the inheritors (see Table 8.1).

Another segment to watch is that of the emerging wealthy, typically those with surplus income as a result of high earnings. Often these are households where there are two high-earning individuals. However,

Table 8.1 Key segments of the UK private banking market

Segment	Key attributes and financial needs
Elderly affluent	Retired, looking for wealth preservation and to be financially secure in old age. Relatively simple banking needs; deposit and savings oriented; low-risk portfolio management geared to income and capital preservation; tax-efficient management including mitigation of inheritance tax.
Inheritors	Often inheriting for the first time from parents, usually a property. Conservative in investment outlook; low-risk investments geared to capital preservation and some steady capital growth.
Retired people	Either: beginning to plan for retirement; usually children are approaching independence. Or: retired, but younger than elderly affluent and some still active in business. More active investments; higher risk tolerance; investment and financial planning oriented.
High income earners	Professionals and senior managers, often working in financial markets. High users of banking products and services including borrowing and cards.
Business owners	Entrepreneurs wanting to expand or sell business. Generally, their personal and business wealth are difficult to separate. High usage of banking products and services including borrowing.

few private banking providers are actively targeting the emerging affluent even though they are the private banking clients of tomorrow.

Wealth distribution

The wealthy are found in a number of geographic concentrations spread unevenly across the UK. A high proportion of wealth is found in the south of England and the home counties surrounding London as well as in concentrated pockets in retirement areas along the coast, in cathedral cities and metropolitan areas. The location chosen by the clearing banks for their offices indicate where the concentrations of wealth are. Offices tend to be much more numerous in the south of England, reflecting the geographic distribution of wealth (see Table 8.2). In this respect, the rapid expansion of private banking offices undertaken by the clearing banks has not been repeated in Scotland given the much smaller scale of the opportunity. The greatest concentrations of high net worth individuals are in the Strathclyde and Grampian areas yet these still remain very much a niche opportunity.

Market needs

The new generation of wealthy are quite distinct from the previous generation in that the new generation is generally more educated and demanding as far as their financial affairs are concerned. These high

Table 8.2 Key locations for private banking offices

London	City of London, Mayfair, West End
Outside London	Oxford, Enfield, Croydon, Abingdon, Richmond, Watford, Bromley
South	Bournemouth, Bristol, Canterbury, Chichester, Eastbourne, Exeter, Guildford, Southampton, Torquay, Truro, Tunbridge Wells, Cheltenham, Plymouth, Worthing
Midlands and East Anglia	Birmingham, Cambridge, Leicester, Norwich, Nottingham, Worcester, Chelmsford
North	Carlisle, Leeds, Liverpool, Manchester, York, Newcastle upon Tyne
South Wales	Cardiff, Swansea
North Wales	Colwyn Bay

net worth individuals have a strong desire to take action with their wealth in a planned and informed way, not leaving their financial future and security to chance, as was more typical of their parents and grandparents. This desire for advice is the single most important thread across an otherwise diverse group of segments.

Financial needs are shaped by significant changes in the economic backdrop. The wealthy and the emerging wealthy are now living in an age of unprecedented economic change in the UK where a number of well-established economic norms have been turned upside down. These are important to understand because they shape and influence the mindset of the marketplace. Some of the key changes have taken place since the late 1980s and can be summarised as:

- **Employment:** During the recession years that started to bite in the early 1990s, unemployment has become prevalent across most socio-economic classes and in most parts of the country, including the affluent south of England. Job security is no longer considered a foregone conclusion, even among the wealthy.
- **Pensions and health:** Where once old age was thought of as secure through government provision, the onus of responsibility has shifted squarely on to the individual to provide comfortably for both healthcare and financial support. Private pension products were introduced into the UK in 1988.
- **Stock market:** Although the UK stock market has been a 'nice little earner', the axiom that markets go up as well as down has come true as demonstrated with the London stock market crash of 1987. It also coincided with a hiatus in privatisation programmes where some investors were investing in equity products for the first time.

- **Property market:** Similarly with property, which experienced a boom in 1987–88, followed by a slump in market prices that lasted until 1996. In the UK, housing has a disproportionate share of personal wealth compared with other markets, and is estimated at 40%.[2]

Compounding these fundamental problems have been events taking place in the financial services arena. Where once the old and trusted financial adviser in the form of a bank manager was the dependable route to take, changes in the way banks operate together with concerns over other financial institutions have left many wealthy individuals unsure as to where to go for trustworthy advice.

The problem with the banks largely started in the mid-1980s and has involved a number of interrelated issues. These have included the years of neglecting the more wealthy customer as banks pursued the mass-market customer; the removal of the traditional bank manager, who was replaced by a less experienced, less autonomous individual; the selling of in-house company products, often perceived as (and often were) inferior compared with the overall market; the belief in the marketplace that the successful selling of these products was more important than the needs of the customer; poor profitability and a long-drawn-out series of poor lending decisions both at home and abroad all helped to blacken the once good reputation of the banks and topple them from their pedestal.

However, few types of institution have remained untouched by market concerns about reputation, whether these relate to the quality of investment advice, the influence of sales targets, commissions paid as a result of sales, the financial stability of an institution, or the huge bonuses earned in the City of London.[3]

Competition

The wealthy in the UK are principally served by UK institutions. Foreign institutions are relegated to niche positions and are normally based in London, being part of worldwide providers such as Citibank and Merrill Lynch, the private banking arms of the Swiss commercial banks or the smaller Swiss banks such as Bank Julius Baer. What is remarkable about the competitive environment is how much it has changed in the 1990s and how the UK banks, particularly the clearing banks, are creating a stir in the market. Now, more than at any other time, there is a huge array of providers of private banking services to choose from (see Table 8. 3).

Table 8.3 Competitor overview of UK private banking marketplace[3]

Banks	Midland Private Banking, Samuel Montagu & Co, Coutts and Co, Barclays Private Bank, Lloyds Private Banking, Adam and Co, Child and Co, Drummond, C Hoare and Co, Private Bank and Trust Co, Arbuthnot Latham, Hambros Private Bank, Duncan Lawrie.
Merchant Banks	Fleming, Kleinwort Benson Private Bank, Lazard Brothers Asset Management, Schroders.
Independent financial advisers (IFAs)	Larger names such as Towry Law; but many more local names.
Stockbrokers	City of London names such as James Capel and Cazenove and a large number of regional brokers.
Investment managers	For example, Mercury Asset Management.
Accountants	Lawyers, accountants, particularly the larger practices including international companies such as Price Waterhouse, tax managers.
Others	Harrods Private Bank.

Providers use different income and investible wealth criteria to identify a private banking client. The clearing banks tend to define the lower threshold of wealth as at least £100 000 (but sometimes less) of investible assets. The London-based merchant banks, asset managers and stockbrokers and more discreet offices within the banks define a private banking client by a higher level of investible wealth level, normally around £1 million. The different levels of wealth criteria reinforce the view of the market as a 'two-horse race'. It is principally the clearing banks that are addressing both markets.

Most of the privately owned banks in the UK have long disappeared or been acquired. The last remaining family-owned bank in the UK with a long tradition is C Hoare and Co. Competition has increased both with banks and non-banks. The major competitor types in domestic private banking are banks, investment managers, independent financial advisers, stockbrokers and accountants.

- Clearing banks, specifically Midland, National Westminster (in the form of Coutts), Barclays and Lloyds, all have domestic private banking arms (as well as international private banking arms). Their key strengths are their financial stability and their access to a vast customer base through the retail banking sector. All offer independent advice.
- An important characteristic of banks such as Duncan Lawrie and Adam and Co is that they are small and this suggests a more personalised service.

- Merchant banks and investment managers are typically London based.
- Independent financial advisers (IFAs) are numerous and found throughout the UK. Their key strength is their ability to provided independent advice, although their size (often small) and receipt of commission payments on products sold can be of concern in some quarters of the high net worth market.
- Stockbrokers are both city and regionally based. Given their focus on stocks and shares, broader financial advice is not generally available. Services are often competitively priced.
- Accountants can be an important referral route of clients to other providers for investment management purposes.

Private banking models

Today, providers of services to the wealthy are distinct in their style of operation, their segmentation approach to the market and their product orientation. The traditional face of private banking has all the hallmarks strongly associated with heritage, tradition and exclusivity. Most of the providers which belong to this small, tightly knit group of merchant banks, stockbrokers and asset managers are based in London.

Sitting alongside the traditional group are the once privately owned banks now with new masters. These include Coutts & Co, Samuel Montagu & Co (owned by Midland Bank), Drummond and Child (both owned by Royal Bank of Scotland). Despite losing their independence they have lost little of the style that denotes their genuine pedigree and tradition. However, despite the family name used by a number of providers, not all are long established in the market and not are they all so financially secure as they seem - witness what happened to Barings. A small group exists which replicates the style but whose pedigree and tradition do not date back nearly so far as those of the genuine once privately owned banks.

Private banking providers generally address the market along product lines with emphasis varying between banking, investments and more specialised asset management services such as estate planning, tax and trusts. The emphasis tends to reflect the product origins of the provider and the market segments on which it focuses:

- Large banks, specifically the clearing banks and Coutts, offer a more universal product approach with a combined breadth and depth of financial services, straightforward banking services, investments, trusts and estate planning.

- Stockbrokers, merchant banks and fund managers are typically investment oriented and offer a range of high-quality specialised investment services.
- Smaller providers focus on banking and lending and have a more limited investment capability or else, a referral route to a more capable investment provider, often in-house, if they are part of a larger financial services group.

Like all financial products, products offered by private banking institutions are no different in that their design is essentially homogeneous. The key differentiators tend to be depth of product specialisation and breadth of product range. However, more importantly, the reputation and stability of the institution and the private banking manager tends to take precedence when a client is selecting a provider.

Powerful position of the clearing banks

Latterly, the increase in competition has largely been stirred up by the clearing banks that are powerfully poised in the domestic private banking opportunity. Key competitive advantages of the clearing banks include an existing relationship with most wealthy and emerging wealthy individuals through their banking relationship; the resources to offer a comprehensive product range; and an existing network within which private banking outlets can operate nationwide. For the clearing banks, the private banking opportunity is twofold: firstly, there is the opportunity to develop a quality fee-income stream and secondly, the opportunity to undertake a vital defensive move to protect their affluent customers from predators.

Despite the slow-moving culture of banks and their aversion to change, the clearing banks in the UK have made significant strides in clawing their way back to within striking distance of the position of respect they once held. Part of this has been the rising standards of servicing and not least the building of a domestic private banking franchise with the wealthy who, while being important profit contributors, are also powerful opinion formers in the marketplace. However, the banks are not homogeneous in their approach to the market and have taken distinctive routes to address the opportunity:

- Midland Bank, now owned by the Hongkong Shanghai Banking Corporation (HSBC) has principally two domestic private banking arms in the UK. Samuel Montagu & Co is a discreet office based in Mayfair, London and focuses on the very wealthy and provides specialist banking and lending services. The larger domestic private banking service operates within the retail bank, Midland Private Banking, started in 1994, which focuses more on the middle tier of wealth. Comprehensive wealth management services are offered by dedicated private banking teams in a separate network of offices, located within the retail bank, throughout the UK.

- Lloyds Bank was the first of the clearing banks to start competing in 1992 for a share of the domestic private banking opportunity and Lloyds Private Banking has been highly successful. Like Midland, comprehensive wealth management services are offered although specialist banking services are reserved for the wealthier. Lloyds has a separate network of offices from the retail bank branches, throughout the UK. It is probably the only leading provider to actively target the emerging affluent and will accept individuals with investible wealth as low as £75 000.
- Coutts & Co is typical of old-style private banks in that it is still strongly characterised by its long-standing tradition of serving wealthy individuals. It has until recently been banking oriented with a strong focus in London and a small number of locations outside central London. However, it has now undertaken a number of important steps to address the opportunity and has a more investment-oriented service proposition, a larger number of offices and a changed organisational structure. This structure now reflects the more partnership-like nature of professional practices, with hierarchy levelled out and clients allocated to a range of senior managers. Moreover, it has lost some of its organisational independence and is now part of a larger wealth management group within National Westminster.
- Barclays Bank has been one of the late-comers, having formed a new private bank in 1996, incorporating the investment expertise of its merchant bank, Barclays de Zoete Wedd (BZW). The private bank has opted to focus on the higher levels of wealth, typically at least £500 000 of investible assets, and is based in London alongside the more traditional group of private banking providers. With specialisation focused on

Table 8.4 Dimensions of providers of UK domestic private banking services (as at 1995)

Provider	Clients	Funds £ billion	Offices	Profit £ million
Coutts & Co	37 000	6	11	42[1]
Lloyds Private Banking	26 000	6	37	22[2]
Midland Private Banking	10 500	2	30	10*[3]

* Estimate

Notes

[1] *Financial Times*, 27 June 1996, p. 1; *First*, Volume 10, Number 3, Quarterly.

[2] Lloyds TSB Group plc Annual Reports and Accounts 1994; *Investors Chronicle*, 9 February 1996.

[3] 'All that glitters is not gold', *Retail Banker International*, 2 February 1996, p. 8. Of the 10 500 clients, Midland Private Banking have 7 000 investment management clients and 3 500 clients who are using the banking service only so far.

the top end, it leaves the middle-tier wealthy to be served by two distinct entities - its retail bank through its Premier Banking Service and Barclays Trust Co which provides investment management and trust services from a central location in Peterborough.

It is evident from the dimensions of the leading providers compared with the size of the market opportunity that the market is huge and under-penetrated. Whilst longevity in the marketplace certainly plays a part in securing market share, the clearing banks are demonstrating that penetration of the market has a lot to do with recognising the new market opportunity and using their competitive strengths in a focused and aggressive fashion.

Strategies

Domestic private banking in the UK is no different from other private banking markets in that it is essentially a referral business. Providers without an extensive distribution network rely heavily on referrals either from professionals such as accountants and solicitors, where incentives for referrals are commonly found, or from existing customers and their families and connections. The primary focus of referrals within clearing banks is on the existing customer base, using either the nationwide branches to identify potential customers or a dedicated business development team.

Traditionally, London was the centre for advice for the wealthy.

Now that wealth is much more locally based, the provision of financial advice has followed the customer and become much more regionalised too. However, in the context of retail bank branch closures and the innovative development of telephone banking, the expansion of private banking services and outlets within the clearing banks is quite a contrast. Some of the more prominent providers such as Lloyds Private Banking and Midland Private Banking have committed themselves to an extensive network of dedicated offices on the basis that the incremental income that these generate merits the cost of bricks and mortar. Providers such as the City-based merchant banks, asset managers and stockbrokers with a presence limited to London appear not to be concerned about physical remoteness from their customers, believing that their strong position in the private banking marketplace is underpinned by customer loyalty, long family associations and the provision of quality service. Given their niche focus, this may well be the case, but it is not the optimal way to target the middle tier of wealth.

Products and the depth and breadth of the product line depend on the provider's origins and will be either banking oriented, investment oriented or a combination of the two. Investment advice is normally independent which means that in-house investment products have to be sold on the basis that they are demonstrably superior to all comparable products. Pricing continues to offer attractive margins to providers with unit trusts comparing favourably with the US mutual funds and portfolio management typically charged at 1% per annum plus broking.

As with other private banking markets, both domestic and international, judging the investment performance of a private banking provider on a truly objective basis has not been possible. A range of measures exist including historic portfolio performance, portfolio performance against given benchmarks such as the FTSE 100, interest-bearing deposit accounts and inflation. Now, this is beginning to change with the Association of Private Client Investment Managers (APCIMS) and FTSE International introducing formal performance measurement indices, published weekly. Although it is still early days, this performance yardstick has the immediately apparent benefits of greater internal management control for the participants and independently assessed performance for the client, and it can sit alongside the more commonly used benchmarks. One of the major barriers will be getting providers to open up to third-party scrutiny but if market demand for this strengthens, it will be only a matter of time before independent performance measurement is much more open and available. The questions are: whether the market demand exists, whether performance measurement within the UK will go as far as the pension fund industry; and how standardised will investment management become.

Where providers offer routine banking services, these now need to be carefully considered in the light of direct banking where convenient, cost-effective and accessible services are being provided by operators such as First Direct. This type of flexible high-tech but highly personal service has broad appeal, also to private banking clients who are not wedded to high-touch banking services and often opt for a more convenient option and so move their accounts.

Private banking providers have been slow to embrace technology as a support method of servicing customers compared with providers of telephone banking in the mass-market sector. There is still a strong school of thought that believes private banking in the UK will continue to be a high-touch rather than a more high-tech type of service. However, going forward, UK domestic private banking providers might well experience something similar to what is happening in the USA where new market segments are redefining service levels; they expect a technology-based interface and are prepared to pay only for value-added services. Even today, non-value-added services are available more cheaply elsewhere; for example, trading, with the introduction of Sharelink.

Most private banking providers are struggling to achieve visibility in a crowded marketplace. The best-known private bank is Coutts, undoubtedly because of the length of time it has been operating in the UK. However, what is important today is to have the most appropriate image and name for the segments being addressed. The name and reputation of the provider plays an important part. On the one hand, there is a long-standing tradition of using the family name style and there is a stable of providers that support such an approach. In contrast, branding can also be in the reverse style through positive association of a parent group such as Midland Private Banking and Lloyds Private Banking. The single most important benefit of this alternative approach is the implied (and real) financial security, stability and reputation bestowed by the parent. However, overcrowding and differentiation from the consumer's perspective, and projection of a more modern image, are issues yet to be addressed by providers.

Regulation

The UK is one of the most regulated financial markets in the world. Overall, financial services have been through a tremendous phase of deregulation and supervisory reregulation. And the changes continue. The key catalysts have been the 1986 Financial Services Act (FSA)[5] and the creation of the Securities and Investment Board (SIB) which is supported by a number of self-regulating organisations,[6] and which is responsible for authorising firms under the FSA.

Some of the key regulatory issues for domestic private banking providers relate to:

- Provision of investment advice.
- Product orientation of the rules.
- Prospecting and referrals without infringing regulations and voluntary codes of conduct.

Where private banking providers have opted for independent status[7] under the FSA - and almost all have - the regulatory and operational requirements are significant. To ensure competency and to comply with regulatory standards as well as improve the service levels to meet rising standards, providers have radically altered operating structures, changed roles and responsibilities and committed increasing levels of resources to compliance, reflecting the growing number of directives from the self-regulating organisations.

Provision of advice broadly involves regular training and assessment of staff to ensure that they have sufficient technical knowledge and that procedures are followed and appropriate advice provided to clients. This means both assessments by in-house compliance teams and independent auditing. Staff who provide investment advice are franchised at different levels, depending on experience and authorisation. Regulations also cover pre-sales, point of sale and on-going service and are highly prescriptive about assessment of needs, information provided and options for the client to withdraw from financial arrangements.

The level of compliance and the product orientation of the rules are key issues for today and the future in the UK. The product focus of the compliance guidelines seems to run counter to the moves providers are making to replace historic product orientation of service to a client orientation.

Furthermore, particularly for banks, prospecting and referral generation has to operate within a number of parameters, not least those of the regulators, but also the Data Protection Act and the Code of Banking Practice. Issues are varied and some strike at the heart of day-to-day servicing, such as:

- Passing information about clients between legal entities only with the express permission of the client, often preferred in writing.
- Where referrals come from the bank branches, sales targets can be only for introductions of prospective clients.
- Sharing open-ended retail banking systems where access to a potentially much larger population is possible.

The key catalysts of 'Big Bang' and the FSA have brought in an unprecedented level of regulations, those under the FSA being geared to the protection of the personal investor. However, the regulations governing financial services are on the political agenda and the main issue is that of the effectiveness of the rules governing providers and of self-regulation, particularly in the light of continuing breaches across a broad spectrum of financial services.

Profitability

True profitability comparisons among private banking providers are difficult to make, as businesses have an individual make-up. In the past, when complex operating structures existed, particularly in clearing banks which had varying degrees of organisational integration, it is doubtful whether true profitability was known. However, this is unlikely to be the case where the value-centre, profit-centre approach is well entrenched.

For private banking organisations, the whole profitability argument revolves around balancing the income potential with the cost of delivery, particularly the balance between expensive resources and bricks and mortar. The argument becomes somewhat more complex when the balance is between the short-term and the long-term realisation of profit; that is, servicing clients today and at the same time securing those individuals who will be the private banking clients of tomorrow. Where, when and how does the emerging private banking client fit into domestic private banking strategies? Moreover, it is predicted that there will be changes in service propositions when providers start to recognise and respond to the different needs across the segments, particularly when the more active and demanding clients such as entrepreneurs and high-income earners are more universally addressed by providers of all types. These segments will have a different profit potential and product make-up.

For the larger operators, where business ambitions are of a significant scale, operational economies will continue to be important. Flatter operating structures, lean head-office and managerial structures are the norm.[8] Sharing investment research and utilising common securities processing and technology platforms with other areas are cost levers. However, for domestic private banking providers, one of the constant battles is to balance the tide of centralisation and standardisation of services so commonplace in financial services groups today with what the private banking client wants.

Product orientation of providers reflects the product profitability potential, in that the core of domestic private banking in the UK is either investment management or highly specialised banking services. Profit from banking services involving routine transactions for wealthy clients is no longer a central profit stream, not least because of direct banking and changes in market demand.

All providers of private banking services need to understand client profitability better and the key is through management information. The continuing problem among most providers is that the emphasis is on processing account data efficiently rather than providing customer management information. Typically, profitability is known in relation to products, teams or offices and the overall business. Profitability models need to address the current and future client profile, particularly as the market segments will increasingly highlight different servicing requirements. This involves information technology and the requirement for more client-oriented systems.

Conclusions and outlook

It is still early days in the UK domestic private banking revolution. Although there has been much activity on the competitor scene, the true size and scope of the opportunity is not yet fully apparent. With the demographic shifts in the UK, the full scale of the level of investible wealth will become more visible only in the next decade as more wealth is released and passed through generations and the impact of ageing population and the issues relating to pension and healthcare provision are better understood.

The evolution of a greatly enlarged high net worth market means that the traditional retail bank and the traditional private bank have both had to change to appeal to this new kind of wealthy individual. Both will need to change more if the true nature of the opportunity is to be fully addressed.

The current market opportunity represents the tip of the iceberg. The market segments receiving the most attention from providers today is that of the already asset rich. They have a strong desire to take action regarding their wealth, and represent a more straightforward market opportunity then the new, faster-growing and more sophisticated segments that are beginning to emerge alongside their older asset rich counterparts.

The emerging affluent are accumulating wealth in their own right through savings and are not being addressed in any notable way by today's providers of private banking services. They represent a new service challenge involving different products and delivery mix, with possibly some kind of technology interface, and generally a more active service level.

There is no indication that competition is abating. The diverse nature of competitors will continue, driven by the continuing lack of attractiveness of other markets. Most providers which continue to target the most affluent will remain in London and encounter a different type of competitor, including stockbrokers, merchant banks and foreign providers such as Swiss private banks which are committing themselves more fully to the UK domestic private banking market.

Today, private banking services means a totality of financial services without necessarily the historical trappings of exclusivity for this new middle ground of private banking customer. Given this radical departure from the old model, there will be an increasing divide between those private banking providers which target the much higher levels of affluence and those that target the middle ground. Only the clearing banks will address both markets in a significant way.

The regulatory environment will continue to be stringent, although there has been the promise of a lighter touch for those providers which have an exemplary track record.

Table 8.5 Prominent UK providers of domestic private banking services

Provider	**Description and wealth guidelines**
Adam and Co	Targets individual with at least £100 000 income or £150 000 investible assets.[1]
Barclays Private Bank	Targets individuals with at least £1 million of investible assets. Operates out of London.
Citibank	Targets families with at least £5 million of net worth.[2] Focuses on London and the South-East. Uniquely offers an Art Advisory Service.
Coutts and Co	Targets individuals with at least £150 000 of investible assets or £100 000 income per annum.[3] Offers a growing range of financial services whereas it was previously banking oriented. For the very wealthy, provides services from the Campbell office in the Strand, London. Also has corporate business in niche sectors such as media and entertainment. Moving its focus from banking to investments.
Child and Co	Targets individuals with income of £30 000 per annum or £200 000 investible assets.[4]
Duncan Lawrie	Targets investible asset of £100 000.[5]
Robert Fleming Private Bank	Targets individuals with income of at least £40 000 income per annum.[6] Focuses on banking and investments.
Harrods Private Bank	Targets individuals with at least £20 000 income per annum.[7] Offers banking services.
C Hoare and Co	Still a traditional family partnership; referrals through existing clients; two branches in London; focuses on banking and has some commercial banking customers.
Kleinwort Benson Private Bank	Targets individuals with at least £75 000 of investible assets; changing its focus to include banking products.
Lloyds Private Banking	Targets individuals with at least £75 000 of investible assets. Focuses on investments but offers integrated banking and investment management from London.
Midland Private Banking	Targets individuals with at least £100 000 of investible wealth or £100 000 of income per annum. Offers banking and asset management services.
Samuel Montagu & Co	Targets individuals with at least £1 million of investible wealth; financially active individuals.

Notes

[1] 'High rollers, UK private banking services', *The Observer*, 10 November 1995.

[2] *Investors Chronicle*, 9 February 1996, p. 44.

[4, 6] *Financial Mail on Sunday*, 16 June 1996, p. 28.

[3, 5, 7] *The Observer*, 16 June 1996, p. B12.

Notes

1 *Prospektus* (1995).
2 'Another housing boom?' *The Economist*, 18 January 1997, p. 59.
3 'High rollers, UK private banking services', *The Observer*, 10 November 1995.
4 The rising demand for credit in the 1970s gave rise to the debt crisis in 1982 which affected banks' balance sheets, largely by lengthening the maturity structure of their loan books as well as decreasing the value of their assets.
5 The Act was passed in 1986 but the majority of the provisions did not come into force until 29 April 1988. It was enacted as a result of a government-initiated review in July 1981. The Act regulates investment business in the UK.
6 The self-regulating organisations (SROs) are the Personal Investment Authority (PIA), Investment Management Regulatory Organisation (IMRO) and the Securities and Futures Authority (SFA). In addition, there are recognised professional bodies (RPBs) such as the Chartered Association of Certified Accountants (CACA), Institute of Chartered Accountants (ICA), Insurance Brokers Registration Council (IBRC), Law Society and Institute of Actuaries.
7 Independent status means the provision of advice covering third-party products rather than advice confined to an in-house product range.
8 *Financial Times*, 27 June 1996, p. 1. An example of this in the UK is Coutts and Co, which has reduced its UK workforce by ten per cent and carried out a radical restructuring to introduce a more partnership-style structure; it has also predicted more job cuts to come during 1997.

CHAPTER NINE

USA

Introduction

The USA is the largest domestic private banking market in the world. It is also one of the more advanced markets, with a diversity of providers, a highly segmented marketplace, a breadth and depth of products and services and an intensely competitive operating environment.

Where the USA stands out is in the positioning of banks and non-banks, demonstrating how deregulation has created high levels of competition between provider types and eliminated complacency where a particular type of provider has been dominant, and has also driven providers to be more innovative and responsive to the marketplace.

The wealthy in the USA are often shrewd and performance oriented, interested not necessarily in service frills but in hard evidence of investment results. Common to all advanced domestic private banking markets, and the USA is no exception, is the overall requirement for added-value service along the lines of information, advice and flexibility of service delivery. Most millionaires in the USA are self-made. With self-made wealth comes the departure from an often mistaken image of wealthy individuals as ostentatious, with expensive lifestyles. As in the UK, the wealthy in the USA today are often characterised by a relatively modest lifestyle, few obvious trappings of wealth and a lack of interest in social status.

It is also clear that technology is beginning to come into its own in private banking, where in some segments a strong preference for convenience and control is being expressed, and providers are seeing the profit reality of re-adjusting the balance between remote and personal face-to-face delivery.

Wealth and the wealthy[1]

As in other industrialised countries, levels of personal wealth have grown out of all historical proportions. In the USA, the phenomenon concerns self-made wealth. It has been estimated that North America overall has $4.4 trillion of high net worth assets, just over one-quarter of the world's high net worth individual wealth. The size of the domestic wealth market has been underpinned by the stability of the USA, the strength of the US dollar and the general absence of motivation to move monies offshore, particularly with regard to taxation since worldwide sources of income are taxable.

Assuming that a private banking client is typically defined as having at least $1 million of investible assets, the private banking market dimensions have been estimated along the following lines:

- The number of households with at least $1 million of investible assets have been estimated at 3.9 million. This market has been growing at an average annual rate of 15%.
- The USA is the home to 149 one-billion dollar fortunes.
- There are four times as many US millionaire business owners now than in 1980 and the number of US dollar millionaires is increasing by 16% a year. Some predictions have been made that between 1995 and 2000, there will be a further five million millionaires.

What is particularly significant about personal wealth creation today in the USA is not just the rate of growth but the fact that new wealth is being created primarily through business. To a lesser extent, high levels of savings, particularly for retirement, contribute to the growth of new wealth together with inheritance - it has been estimated that 20% of today's wealthy individuals have benefited from an inheritance.

- **Entrepreneurial wealth:** Small businesses continue to play a large part in the US economy and wealth creation. The early phases of economic development were dominated by family businesses, but there has been a significant growth since the early 1980s of start-up businesses which are estimated to be growing at an average annual rate of 20%. A further change is that today, businesses are typically a major wealth-creation vehicle for the current generation, because businesses are often sold during the lifetime of the owner instead of being passed on. Business start-ups are also increasingly spread across a diversity of low-tech and 'unglamorous' sectors, far beyond the traditional high-tech industry of 'Silicon Valley' that has been the dominant and more highly publicised sector to date.

- **Saving for retirement and the 'baby boomers':** The shift of responsibility to the individual to provide for retirement and the move from corporate pension contributions to employee contributions have constituted another important wealth creation vehicle. Some 50 million Americans now own equities directly or through retirement savings. This is particularly significant in relation to the demographic profile of the USA. The population shows an increasingly ageing profile, thanks to the 'baby boomers' who will start to retire around 2012.

As in many domestic markets, wealth in the USA is heavily regionalised. The larger private banking markets are found in California, Texas, Florida, Washington, New York and Boston. Wealth is found mainly where regional economies are flourishing, and in retirement and metropolitan areas.

Segmentation of wealthy

As in most private banking markets, providers of domestic private banking services use a number of financial criteria ranging from investible assets to annual income and net worth less primary residence. Typically, a private banking client is defined by using a benchmark of investible assets, most commonly $1 million as a minimum level. However, a number of bank providers are beginning to revise their segmentation strategy and now recognise the importance of the emerging affluent as a market for private banking services today. By including them, banks can strengthen their customer franchise by supporting the client during the early stages of wealth creation with the hope of reaping the benefit when the individual becomes asset rich.

There are four broadly defined markets within the US domestic private banking market:

- **Emerging affluent**, including, for example, professionals, corporate executives and high-income earners.
- **Entrepreneurs**, including, for example, business owners developing their business, entrepreneurs who have sold their business and entrepreneurs starting out who are seeking to accumulate wealth.
- **Retired**, typically wealth protectors who are already asset rich.
- **Super wealthy**, including very wealthy families and individuals.

Financial profile of the wealthy

Households with investible wealth exceeding $1 million would typically have the following financial profile:[2]

- Investible assets would account for approximately 70% of wealth and be invested in a range of assets including deposits, mutual funds, direct equity portfolio, trusts, individual stocks and bonds.
- The remaining 30% of the portfolio would predominantly reflect equity in real estate including the principal residence, an investment in real estate as well as possibly in a privately owned business, and some insurance, see Fig. 9.1.

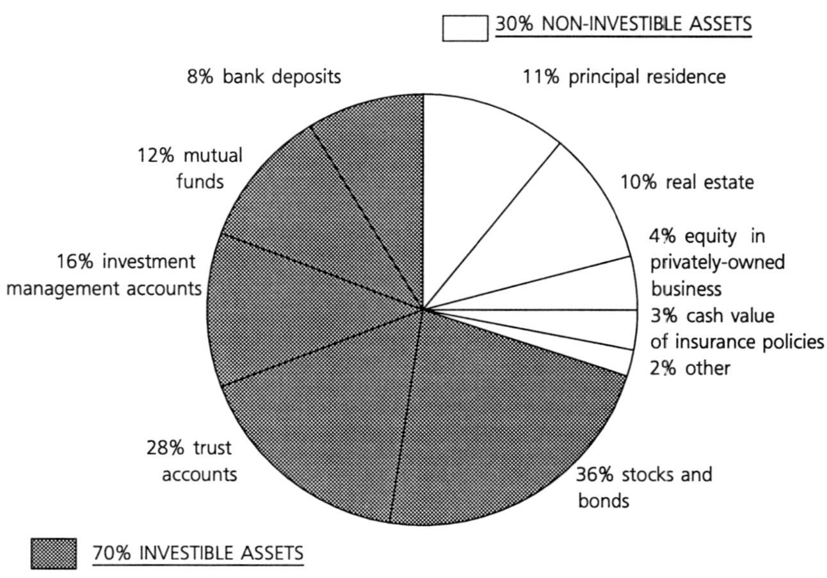

Figure 9.1 Financial profile of the wealthy.

Source: PSI

Needs of the wealthy

Wealthy individuals are beginning to influence the market now perhaps more than at any other time, causing providers, to change their traditional *modus operandi* - banks, which have traditionally been high-touch with a one-service-fits-all approach, and non-banks which typically are high-tech and execution oriented. It means that the private banking market with its different segments requires a diversity of approach, implying that providers with a single delivery will need to either focus on the segment that wants that kind of service or else have multiple-service propositions in order to service a broader market.

The forces at work among the wealthy relate to three key areas:

- **Provider orientation and the number of provider relationships:** The number of relationships that a wealthy individual might have now varies according to the complexity of needs and the type of services sought. What is clear is that a vast number of private banking clients have multiple relationships spanning different provider types, making share of wallet an increasingly difficult objective to achieve.
- **The complexity of an affluent customer's needs:** This depends on a number of variables including life stage, wealth levels, financial sophistication and needs. The product solutions can vary enormously from a simple single investment or trust solution to active stock broking and to a much more specialised and sophisticated range of services that perhaps an investment bank might provide.
- **The value that the customer attaches to different services:** It is clear that certain segments are redefining the service levels, with dissatisfaction in some segments about the traditional way of servicing and value attributed to certain services only. The changes have been triggered largely by the high-quality and low-cost mutual fund providers and the advancements of technology which provide increasing low-cost access to certain financial transactions, such as on-line share dealing, without the intermediation of a financial institution or a private banker.

These changes are segmenting the market along provider, customer needs and product lines. Nevertheless, the demand for advice and service remains constant for wealthy individuals. What is now clear is that private banking is no longer exclusively a high-touch, low-tech

	PROVIDER ORIENTED	PRODUCT ORIENTED
HIGH COMPLEXITY	**Need**: Integrated advisory service **Value**: $750 000 investible assets 27% of market	**Need**: Flawless access High end products **Value**: $650 000 investible assets 21% of market
LOW COMPLEXITY	**Need**: Simple relationship **Value**: $244 000 Investible assets 34% of market	**Need**: Access and convenience **Value**: $218 000 Investible assets 18% of market

* Affluent is defined as those households with more than $75 000 in income or more than $300 000 in net worth

Figure 9.2 Matrix of affluent clients based on complexity of needs and orientation.
Source: Oliver, Wyman and Company; PSI; Forum research

service. The one-size-fits-all idea, namely the automatic provision of a personal relationship manager, is no longer appropriate for all.

Competition

Traditionally, wealthy individuals were provided with lending or investment services by banks, either money-centre banks or regional banks. Often, these services were provided by separate departments within the bank: namely the private banking, investment and trust departments. These three areas within the banks rarely came together to service the client in a co-ordinated fashion, instead keeping within their product lines.

With increased deregulation which allowed non-bank entrants into the financial services arena, banks have long lost their exclusive product and customer franchise with the wealthy. The wealthy now have an extensive choice of providers, many of which compete on price and service and have virtually identical product capability. Over the last decade, mutual fund providers and brokerage houses have become the most dominant and aggressive providers in the private banking market, excelling at marketing, developing innovative products and delivering high-quality service.

The wealthy in the USA are principally served by US institutions. Foreign banks have yet to make any significant inroads in the marketplace. Where present, foreign entrants, generally European, are mainly trying to appeal to US wealthy individuals who are interested in greater international diversification.

As in the UK, the competitive environment in the USA is diverse and fragmented (see Table 9.1).

Providers competing for a share of private wealth range from banks, mutual fund companies, brokerage firms and investment boutiques to asset managers and, more recently, independent financial planners who are able to provide objective and independent advice on any products in the market, thereby competing with non-banks which typically provide their own in-house range (see Table 9.3).

Table 9.1 Competitive overview in the USA

Provider type	**Key providers**
Bank	First Union, KeyCorp, PNC, Northern Trust, Wachovia, Bank of Boston, Bank of America, Wells Fargo, Mellon Bank, Republic National Bank of New York, Chase Manhattan Bank, Bankers Trust, Bessemer Trust, US Trust Corporation, NationsBank, Harris Trust
Investment banks	Goldman Sachs, JP Morgan
Brokerages	Merrill Lynch, Smith Barney
Discount brokerages	Charles Schwab
Privately owned bank	Riggs, Brown Brothers Harriman
Mutual fund companies	Fidelity, Vanguard
Investment boutiques	Numerous
Foreign banks	Union Bank of Switzerland, Crédit Suisse, Swiss Bank Corporation Deutsche Bank, Coutts

Table 9.2 Primary focus of provider types

Provider type	**Focus (investible assets of client)**
Investment banks	>$5 million
Money-centre banks	$2–5 million
Super-regional banks	$0.5–2 million
Full-service brokerages	$0.2–0.5 million
Mutual fund companies	<$0.5 million

Competitive focus

Whilst there is increasing fluidity within market segmentation and financial criteria, the various types of provider focus on specific levels of wealth in the private banking market, although some shifts are detectable today (see Table 9.2).

There is evidence that brokerages are gaining share of the higher wealth levels, traditional bank territory, where individuals have at least $1 million of investible assets. Fragmentation in the marketplace means that share of wallet is increasingly difficult and is spread between brokerages, mutual fund companies and banks. With the increase in multiple relationships, the issue of who is primary provider is difficult to determine.

Dominance of non-banks[3]

The mutual fund companies and the brokerage firms represent the single most important threat to banks in the management of private wealth. Inter-bank competition still tends to be largely regionalised because of the historical restrictive development of inter-state banking. Within the more localised competitive environment are the numerous investment boutiques which are generally renowned for providing highly personal service and which compete for trust and investment business.

At a nationwide level, the mutual fund companies and brokerages firms present formidable opposition to the banks, none of which can be described as nationwide yet. The biggest mutual fund company in the USA (and the world, for that matter) is Fidelity. Brokerage firms too are impressive money managers and some, such as Merrill Lynch and Smith Barney, have extensive sales forces. The key advantages that mutual fund companies and brokerage firms have over banks are their low-cost products, innovative and extensive investment product ranges and sales and marketing expertise.

The following figures (not confined to domestic private banking) are indicative of the overall size and presence of non-banks:

- The brokerage industry earned pre-tax income of $13 billion in 1996.
- Size of client assets managed have been estimated as follows – Merrill Lynch $830 billion; Fidelity $500 billion and Charles Schwab $253 billion.
- Merrill Lynch has 13 600 financial consultants and Smith Barney 10 400.

Retaliation by the banks[4]

Some banks, particularly those with a long history and established reputation, have been able to hold their position in servicing the wealthy. On the whole, though, banks have had to address the impact of deregulation, growing competition and some inherent cultural characteristics.

Deregulation has meant that while non-banks have marched ahead in the provision of investment products, banks have had to try to catch up with the brokerage firms and mutual fund companies by acquiring investment expertise, a range of investment products and building a name for themselves as money managers. Although most of this has been achieved, it is the demonstrable investment performance and track record of the non-banks which continues to overshadow banks.

For many wealthy individuals, the traditional bank relationship has become fragmented. With deregulation allowing non-banks to develop their product range so extensively as to be virtually identical to a bank product range, the bank relationship has been undermined as customers buy products and services elsewhere and have multiple relationships. The issue for the banks is how to guard their more wealthy clients, particularly those who are already asset rich, from non-banks as inevitably the asset-rich segments become common marketing ground between the bank and non-bank. At the same time, the banks are now recognising the emerging affluent and the importance of strengthening and building up their initial banking relationship before the non-bank providers can reach them and entice them away. The issues of life-time value and understanding client profitability are even more critical with these yet-to-be established affluent individuals.

Changing *modus operandi* of both banks and non-banks[5]

In the 1980s, banks started to review and change their traditional *modus operandi*. This has involved a number of structural and cultural changes. Some of the key ones have been:

- Integrating the private banking, trust and brokerage units.
- Eliminating certain long-standing roles such as that of the trust and loan officer and creating broader roles focusing on relationship management with product specialist support.
- Introducing training programmes on service and sales.

- Designing performance measures and incentives to reflect sales management and growth.
- Shifting the traditional expertise of technical and procedural competence to a more highly developed skill base that emphasises sales and service.

Some of this is still happening today and the super-regional banks are particularly active in introducing the changes required to better serve the wealthy.

While the banks have been getting their house in order so as to address the competition, mutual fund companies and brokerage firms have continued to grow and flourish. At the end of 1995, there were 5761 mutual funds managed by 401 different companies. However, more recently, they too have been having to revisit their traditional method of operating within the private banking marketplace. The main traditional sources of income have been transaction services, often utilising remote delivery methods such as the telephone, but now the mutual fund companies and brokerage houses are recognising that transaction services and the income derived from them are coming under threat from changes in market needs.

Non-banks have clearly recognised the threat of the development of on-line brokerage execution and that their service proposition is increasingly susceptible to product commoditisation where on-line trades can cost $15 a transaction. There is now a noticeable move towards providing more advice and information with a financial planning focus. Additionally, to support the provision of advice, mutual fund providers, such as Fidelity, are extending their advice centres and beginning to address the issue of relationship management, a departure from the traditional remote-servicing, execution-only capability. It is also evident that Schwab is expanding its services to include investment planning and performance analytics.

Foreign competition[6]

Given the immense size of the personal wealth pool generated by the USA, it is not surprising that foreign providers continue to try and nibble away at the private banking opportunity, despite the over-crowded nature of the competitor arena. To date, such crowding has allowed nothing more than a highly selective focus and presence. Presence in New York, Miami, Chicago, Los Angeles and San Francisco is also undoubtedly in support of dual strategies – from these metropolitan areas, international private banking services are provided for cross-border wealth from Latin America, Mexico, Canada and Asia. It appears, though, that global private banking players consider it essential to have a presence and some activity, no matter how small in the US marketplace, which demonstrates the importance of the USA as an integral part of a global private banking strategy.

Strategies[7]

For banks overall, the challenge is to halt and reverse the trend of non-banks increasing their penetration of the private banking market. In 1994, US bank share of financial services provided to the wealthy (with at least $1 million of investible assets) dropped from 34% to 23%, while brokerage firms increased their share from 31% to 38%. The issue (and the opportunity) for banks is how to make the most of one of their more significant competitive advantages over non-banks; an existing customer base with the natural product franchise of a bank account, car loan or credit card. A further topical issue is how to galvanise the internal workings of the bank and overcome turf and cultural issues to ensure a steady flow of referrals to the private banking unit - hence the major structural changes that have been taking place across the bank sector.

For non-banks, growth has been founded on hunting rather than farming to acquire a customer base. Excellent marketing, economic remote servicing channels and, in the case of brokerage houses, extensive and productive sales forces, have all contributed to the aggressive and profitable growth of non-banks. With sizeable customer bases, non-banks are beginning to farm these, introducing new products such as trusts. Much has been made of the cultural differences between banks and non-banks, particularly brokerage houses, and it is undoubtedly in the field of sales that the brokerage houses have demonstrated a clear lead over the banks.

While banks have physical distribution through their branch network, non-banks, particularly the brokerage houses, have geographic coverage thanks to technology and a mobile sales force. Bank providers of private banking services are having to compete with nationwide providers such as Fidelity, which has approximately 82 investment centres across 30 states. However, because of changing customer needs, a middle ground is starting to emerge where the balance between face-to-face servicing and remote servicing is altering. For banks, the shift has been towards the increased use of technology and remote servicing, thereby meeting clients' needs more effectively and improving profitability where the more costly traditional private banker formula was formerly the norm. Further bank developments have been the establishment of tele-servicing centres, often for trusts where only a simple service is required. Increasingly, on-line services are being planned and some have already been developed in recognition of clients' need for information, convenience and control over their affairs.

Technology will play an increasing part in the future of private banking in the USA. Today, personal computer based packages are already being made available to clients. The Internet is increasingly a forum for suppliers and buyers - 75% of Web users live in North America and it is fast becoming an interactive medium. It has also been predicted that nearly one in six American households will be banking over the Internet within the next four years and most of them will be relatively well off and account for at least one-third of bank profits. Services on-line will be expanded to include, for example, bill payment, management of share portfolio and the buying of pension schemes over the Web. It seems more than likely that private banking will increasingly feature on-line services for certain segments and aspects of the market.

Most providers have started with a traditional product orientation; many have recognised the need to re-balance product and income streams. Banks are re-balancing towards investments, having been by far the dominant providers of trusts and credit, they have the largest market share of trust business overall in the USA, with 42% compared with brokerages which have a reported 8% of trust assets under management. Investment boutiques are strong in investments and trusts and mutual fund companies and brokerage firms are leading investment product providers. Generally, all providers of private banking services have expanded beyond their traditional strengths, helping to blur product demarcation lines.

Bank providers have not generally been renowned for product innovation (perhaps not helped by the regulatory environment at certain times) and have tended to be followers rather than leaders in product development. Innovation has emanated mainly from the mutual fund companies and brokerage firms. However, banks are now recognising that they have to be more innovative with their products, particularly with the emerging affluent segment. In order to address this segment and to respond to the growing requirement for information and financial planning, they have developed value-added products such as cash management accounts and wrap accounts with mutual funds, all increasingly commonplace in the product range of banks in the USA today.

Segmented product approaches are also now well established and have evolved according to a typical formula in that the top tier of wealthy are provided with a dedicated relationship manager and an individually tailored proposition, including discretionary portfolio management; the emerging wealthy are offered a more packaged solution involving mutual funds rather than a bespoke investment portfolio. The formula reflects the economies and profitability of asset gatherers in comparison with the asset rich.

Some examples of segmented service approaches are:

- Mellon Bank through its subsidiary Dreyfus Corporation has developed Dreyfus Masterpiece, an asset management service, for individuals who have between $200 000 and $1 million to invest.
- Chase Manhattan Bank provides clients who have at least $1 million of investible assets with the traditional bespoke one-to-one service through its private banking unit. Clients are typically wealthy families many of whom were clients of the bank's trust division, and entrepreneurs whose main relationship has been through a lending officer. Those clients with investible assets of between $500 000 and $1 million are offered the Chase Manhattan Investment Services group, which is the retail bank's brokerage arm.
- KeyCorp, one of the leading super-regional banks, provides three private banking programmes reflecting market groupings: Private Banking and Investing for the emerging affluent and Wealth Management for families with at least $2 million of investible assets.

One of the consistent features of private banking whether domestic or international, is the essential ingredient of reputation. This is true of the USA as elsewhere. Pre-eminent providers which have a reputation based on longevity and competence tend to have a cachet associated with pedigree and tradition, much on the model of European private banks. Typical providers with this type of cachet include US Trust, JP Morgan, Brown Brothers Harrison, Harris Trust, Northern Trust and Chase Manhattan Bank.

For relatively newer providers of private banking services, particularly for the non-bank population, reputation is typically built on product performance and service excellence. Importantly, in the private banking arena, it depends on the ability to provide investment expertise. It is the mutual fund companies and brokerage houses which have outclassed banks and have the reputation for being aggressive money managers.

For today's affluent in the USA, banks (with a few exceptions) are not generally perceived as the leaders in investment, though they have made significant strides in catching up with the non-bank competition. Investment and mutual fund expertise has been gained through acquisitions and by building the capability in-house so that private banking units have access to expertise for their clients - although generally third-party investment products are also introduced.

However, there is still a strong perception in the market that banks are inferior money managers, despite the fact that they have managed significant trust monies for decades. The inescapable truth and conundrum for banks is that it is hard to market investment expertise if the fund performance track record is short. Moreover, where banks have a better shot at promoting their track record, they have not been allowed to advertise performance of common funds (typically aggregated trusts).

As always, there are two sides to the story. While the banks, which were bestowed with high levels of trust by the market, have to convince the market that they too can be aggressive money managers, brokers also have aspects of reputation and image to address. Even though they have shifted their positioning from broker to financial planner, questions are still posed regarding the objectivity of their advice, given the proprietary nature of their products together with their remuneration structure, which undoubtedly reinforces the transaction and product focus of their sales thrust.

Regulation and legislation[8]

For much of banking history in the USA, banks have been shaped by regulation which has defined their product, price and geographic boundaries. Regulation has not only increased competition but has also been a major factor behind revenue erosion for the banks and loss of their deposit base. It was not until the repeal of Regulation Q (finally in 1982) that banks were able to compete with non-bank money market mutual funds and achieve a more level competitive playing field. However, with the repeal of this regulation, a permanent increase in price competition together with the banks' cost of interest and credit shortage in the 1980s had a devastating impact on bank margins, profitability and market share.

In response, banks expanded their product ranges to stem the deposit outflow and restructured their business portfolio. The strategic rationale involved generating better quality earnings and developing a mix of high-value-creating businesses such as private banking, trust and asset management (amongst other business lines).

Certainly, deregulation has created a highly competitive environment and views continue to be expressed about the unevenness of the playing field. For banks, there are indeed significant hurdles to be crossed with regard to the various licensing requirements for different products. This has given an added complexity to the structural changes undertaken in private banking in which products and people have been integrated into a single sales and servicing function. At the same time, the disclosure rules differ, too; for example, there are less intensive disclosure requirements for mutual funds than for trusts. But the view has also been expressed that banks have been also partly protected by regulation too, particularly where deposits, payment systems and lending are concerned.

With 'Know Your Customer' regulations expected from the Federal Reserve Bank, increased monitoring of clients and relationships is expected to replace the current requirement for banks to report all transactions over $10 000.

Profitability[9]

Economies are achievable when the provider is part of a larger organisation, as is the case for most providers of private banking services. Product manufacturing, back-office processing and technical expertise are areas for common utilisation.

Super-regionals are becoming increasingly reliant on profit from their private units because of the stagnant state of the mass market.

Banks overall have been trying to re-balance their revenue streams; the development of private banking particularly towards a more investment orientation is part of this overall policy. Certainly, revenue from investments are growing at a fast rate. Non-interest income from fees and trading as a proportion of American commercial banks' total income rose from an average of 19% in 1960–80 to 35% in 1994.

In common with all private banking businesses, in all countries, domestic private banking in the USA has a high cost base attributable to people. The expenses relate to quality of people, ensuring technical expertise is in place and providing training to meet licensing requirements.

Greater sophistication has been achieved in assessing the profitability of clients and their lifetime revenue potential. This has included going beyond the level of financial assets held to include the servicing costs and sales process involved in order to achieve a complete history of the profit model of individual clients. This then enables decision to be made, including those involving disinvestment or at least change of delivery mechanism to a less costly one. It also helps banks identify and defend those clients who contribute the profit; some estimates indicate that 10% of clients contribute 90% of profit.

Conclusions and outlook

The USA is the largest domestic private banking marketplace worldwide, with just under four million households with investible assets of at least $1 million. With high levels of growth (15% per annum) and increasing wealth distribution, it is now also a much more segmented market than hitherto, with business owners and the emerging affluent representing two of the most significant market opportunities.

Providers of domestic private banking services are mostly US institutions although some of the larger and most international of foreign institutions, principally European, operate in a small way out of the highly competitive metropolitan areas. They have had very limited success to date in penetrating the market.

The wealthy were traditionally served by banks but this is no longer the case. Today, mutual fund providers and brokerage houses are the most dominant and aggressive providers in the US domestic private banking marketplace and have excelled at marketing, developing innovative products and delivering high quality service.

Consequently, the wealthy are besieged by a diversity and depth of competition. Most bank and non-bank providers have diversified their products and services beyond traditional boundaries to the point that, today, there is little product category differentiation.

In addressing the wealthy, banks have developed and changed considerably, undertaking major structural and cultural reforms and this is particularly true of the super-regional banks. Investment expertise has been acquired or built in-house; product and service ranges have been developed and tiered to defend and develop their high net worth customer base, and all within an onerous regulatory environment.

However, there are some major changes under way in the needs of the wealthy, relating to three areas; provider selection and number of provider relationships; complexity of customer needs; and the value

Table 9.3 Prominent providers of domestic private banking services in the USA

Provider	Description
Bank of America	Targets individuals with at least $1 million of investible assets; also has an international private banking strategy. Estimated to manage a total of about $50 billion of client assets.
Bank of Boston	Targets individuals with at least $1 million of investible assets; full service range; an East Coast bank based in Boston.
Bessemer Trust	Targets individuals with at least $5 million of investible assets; long-standing reputation in private banking market; based in Chicago; started as family office.
Brown Brothers Harriman	One of the few privately owned, unlimited liability partnerships, founded in 1818.
Chase Manhattan Bank	Targets individuals with at least $1 million of investible assets; East Coast money-centre bank based in New York.
Fidelity	Largest mutual fund company in the world with $400 billion of funds under management of approximately 200 mutual funds.
Harris Trust	Strong reputation in private banking market; based in Chicago.
KeyCorp	Tenth-largest bank in USA; mid-West super-regional bank based in Cleveland; targets emerging affluent as well as core affluent and super-wealthy families.
Mellon Bank	West Cost bank based in California.
Merrill Lynch	Full-service brokerage house; nationwide.
JP Morgan	'Blue blood' investment bank targeting individuals with at least $5 million of investible assets; based East Coast.
NationsBank	Fourth-largest bank in USA; 26 private banking offices; super-regional bank.
Northern Trust	Leading provider based in Illinois; long-standing reputation in private banking market particularly in trusts.
PNC	Targets individuals with at least $1m of investible assets; super-regional bank based in Pittsburgh.
Republic National Bank of New York	Targets individuals with at least $1 million of investible assets; East Coast bank.
Riggs	Based in Washington.
Charles Schwab	Largest discount brokerage house in USA; nationwide.
Smith Barney	Full-service brokerage house.
US Trust Corporation	'Blue blood' bank; long-standing reputation in private banking market; full service range.
Vanguard	Mutual fund company.
Wells Fargo	Bank based on West Coast.

attached to services by the customer. While delivery is going through some major changes, what has not gone away is the demand for information, advice and added-value service, whether the provider is a bank or non-bank.

Technology will play an increasing part in the service proposition of private banking providers, depending on the segment. The growth of personal computer ownership, expansion of the Internet and increasing demand for convenience and flexibility are bound to continue.

Relying on traditional strengths whether as a bank or non-bank is no longer strategically appropriate in the private banking marketplace. Providers with traditional remote delivery are developing alternatives including face-to-face delivery. Income which traditionally has been sourced through transaction commission is increasingly vulnerable and fee-based income is being sought for more advisory type services.

Banks still face the uphill struggle of convincing the market that they can be aggressive money mangers like their non-bank counterparts.

The regulatory environment has fostered high levels of competition across financial services, albeit providing, at the same time, varying degrees of protection to provider types.

Profitability for private banking providers will be linked increasingly to how a customer is served. Delivery and the cost of serving the customer are coming increasingly under the microscope and tiered products and alternative delivery channels are emerging. Technology will play an increasingly visible role in the customer relationship as well as in administrative support, reflecting both cost and market requirements.

It has been predicted that there will be 15–20 dominant domestic private banking providers, both bank and non-bank, in the USA by the turn of the century, possibly sooner given the changes already taking place in the financial services industry involving acquisitions and mergers. Non-bank providers will continue to make inroads in the higher wealth segments, where individuals have at least $1 million of investible assets.

Notes

1 *World Wealth Report 1997*, Gemini Consulting and Merrill Lynch.
Interview with Payment Systems Inc., 1996.
Retirement savings are largely in two forms; 41(k)s are a money purchase pension and Individual Retirement Accounts (IRAs) were introduced in 1981 and are personal pension plans. Quarterly Review of Personal Finance, *Financial Times*, 18 and 19 October 1996.
Forbes, 15 July 1996.

Retail Banker International, 2 February 1996, p. 8; 'How banks can grow along with the trust market', *American Banker*, 11 September 1995, p. 11.

2 Interview with Payment Systems Inc., 1996.

3 *Forbes*, 10 February 1997.

4 *American Banker*, 22 June 1995, p. 1. Merrill Lynch, one of the leading full-service brokerage firms, started its first trust operation in 1987; today, most of its trust clients are existing clients of Merrill Lynch with trust assets under management totalling $27 bn.

5 Quarterly Review of Personal Finance, *Financial Times*, 18 and 19 October 1996.

6 European providers which have strengthened their commitment to the market include a number of Swiss providers such as Bank Julius Baer, Union Bancaire Privée and Union Bank of Switzerland.

7 'Retool your private bank unit to meet the non-bank threat', *American Banker*, 13 February 1996, p. 11.

It has been estimated that the average private banker spends 10–15% of total time on business development compared with non-bank competitors which spend 40–60%. *American Banker*, 13 February 1996, p. 11.

'The Internet grows out of nappies', *The World in 1997*, *The Economist*, p. 115.

'Intuitively competitive', *The Economist*, 21 December 1996, p. 108.

American Banker, 22 June 1995, p. 1.

The cash management account (CMA) often considered one of the most innovative personal banking products, was first developed by Merrill Lynch in 1977. The product allowed non-banks to provide what had been traditional bank services. The Merrill Lynch CMA provided money-market mutual funds with a cheque book, brokerage facilities and margin borrowing.

'Targeting emerging wealth', *Private Banker International*, October 1995, p. 9.

A number of notable investment acquisitions have been made within the bank population. KeyCorp acquired Spear, Benzak, Salomon and Farrel; Mellon Bank acquired First Boston and Dreyfus; PNC acquired Black Rock Finance.

8 Regulation Q was brought in under the Banking Act of 1935, whereby the Federal Reserve was given power to establish maximum interest rates that banks could pay on various savings and time deposits. This was later abolished (albeit on a phased basis) and in 1982 the Garn St Germain Act (1982) granted banks with money-fund-equivalent powers. John B. McCoy, Larry A. Frieder, Robert B. Hedges, Jr *BottomLine Banking*, 1994.

The 1933 Banking Act, popularly known as the Glass-Steagall Act, created the Federal Deposit Insurance Corporation (FDIC). It became the official agency to protect bank depositors. Banks were prohibited from operating across state lines, selling or underwriting securities or engaging in non-financial activities. The original rationale behind the regulations was to stabilise the banking system after a series of banking crises up to the 1930s. Lowell L. Bryan *Breaking the Bank*, 1988, p. 4.

9 'US money laundering regulations expected', *Private Banker International*, December 1996.

US Trust Corporation transformed its balance sheet from nearly 100% commercial banking to exclusively private banking and trust services, achieving 79% of revenues from fee income. *American Banker*, 7 April 1995, p. 8.

CHAPTER TEN

Industry outlook

Introduction[1]

This concluding chapter reviews the issues that the private industry faces over the medium and long term. The challenges described are faced by both international and domestic private banking. The successful private banking providers of the future will be the ones that can coherently tackle:

- The effects of globalisation.
- Information technology.
- Service quality and business standards.
- New competencies and measures of success.

Private banking is now dealing with the consequences of being a phenomenon of the financial services industry. The trend so far is towards investment, support and expectation of high profit contribution. The delivery of the latter in already being called for particularly in the case of the universal providers which are being forced to change their revenue mix due to other poor performing business sectors often suffering from income stream volatility or market maturity.

Globalisation[2]

Globalisation is principally an economic and political force directed at free trade and has as byproducts job and wealth creation, price competitiveness and development of markets worldwide. In the private banking context, money is one of the most global commodities and private banking is affected by globalisation, which allows people, ideas, information and capital to move freely across borders. When digital in form, wealth can leave jurisdictions and be invested worldwide almost instantaneously. Evidence of global forces already affecting the industry has been identified in previous chapters, for example:

- The re-balancing of worldwide wealth regionally.
- Client behaviour undoubtedly influenced by information, international education and travel, and the new generation of wealthy ringing the changes in service requirements.
- The continuing flow of wealth across international jurisdictions as well as between onshore and offshore.
- The increasingly international investment profiles of private wealth.

Yet, despite these trends that indicate the convergence of a number of global themes, private bankers both international and domestic have to address a number of countervailing forces.

- **Wealth is still highly localised** and wealth creation is found in concentrated pockets worldwide such as in Hong Kong, Singapore, South-East China, Bangalore, California, Tokyo and the South-East of England. Although private banking can be considered a global business, it remains a business that needs to be highly focused in its targeting and the location of its operations.
- **Although wealth can flow freely across borders, local and regional tensions are still dominant.** Fiscal barriers are significant forces opposing an otherwise growing international tide of regulations and legislation by bodies such as the G7, BIS and the EU that address worldwide concerns such as money laundering and banking confidentiality. Taxation represents are important local tension for wealth management purposes and is likely to remain so. Diversity of

taxation not only at the domestic level but also within offshore jurisdictions is now on the international agenda. However, the unevenness found across jurisdictions is likely to prevail for some time, given the vested national interests in maintaining the *status quo*. To date, arguments on diversity of taxation are based largely on differences across geographic jurisdictions given that geography is key to collection of taxes and the determining of tax liability. This is now rapidly being overtaken by the need also to address cyberspace and electronic commerce where transactions are already crossing borders and jurisdictions, deeming geography irrelevant.

- **Local governments will also continue to have tight control over financial services.** Regulations will persist in protecting markets, blocking foreign competition and creating distinctive financial services arenas. Addressing the liberalisation of financial markets is the General Agreement on Tariffs and Trade (GATT), with the General Agreement on Trade in Services (GATS) reviewing financial services. Liberalisation, although a number of countries are committed to it, is likely to be a slow process of evolution tailored to national objectives – rightly so in some senses, given that deregulation of markets needs to be tightly controlled and managed.
- **Dual domestic and international strategies will become increasingly commonplace.** But the importance of a recognisable name and, in some markets, the local franchise, will be a major competitive strength. While the larger universal providers from within global financial services can gain access to markets with comparative ease, medium-size and smaller providers have the opportunity to be more innovative in their approach to markets and can pursue partnerships, alliances and joint ventures to expand their market focus and product capability. Well-recognised global brands will continue to be important and will have different resonances in different markets. The success of global names will continue to depend on the strength of local competition.

Impact of information technology[3]

A growing trend across financial services is to scrutinise the spend on information technology (IT). Already, analysts studying overcapitalisation in the banking industry are recognising that the spend on technology must be examined more closely, not least because of expenditure that was committed in the 1970s and 1980s. Key areas for the future are linking spend to quantifiable benefits; unit costs; lag of management know-how behind technology advances; and automated processes in the absence of re-engineering.

Overall bank spending on technology, specifically that of the US commercial banks, has been rising year on year since 1987. The spend trend is reflected in private banking where it is estimated that IT is the second-largest element of costs in private banking, behind personnel, and on average accounts for 12% of operating costs. Although spending is predicted to rise, the increase is relatively modest given the scope of the tasks to be undertaken. In the future, IT will be significant in a number of areas from service delivery and product management to revenue generation and facilitating changes in strategic direction.

- **A more innovative delivery and service:** There is already an evident trend in new market segments towards a preference for an alternative service delivery channel using personal computers (complementing telephones and faxes), suggesting that a higher degree of technology interface will be introduced into the service proposition. Particularly with the growing ownership of computers, a broader spectrum of service delivery combining face-to-face service and remote service is possible. The virtual private banker and video conferencing with clients are not such far-fetched ideas. The point, though, is that technology is already influencing how and where high net worth individuals get access to wealth management services and that high-touch personal service will be just one rather than the only one way of delivering service to wealthy individuals.

- **The growing force of the Internet:** Already, private banking providers are recognising its potential and are utilising the Internet by creating Web sites and providing static data such as pricing, company reports and fund performance. The Internet is a medium that is helping to make available information that was previously held within opaque industries. Key developmental areas are making money digital, paperless transactions and instant flows of information. However, the Internet is still relatively unfamiliar and often viewed as a threat even though core skills of a private banking provider, such as lending money, gathering assets and managing assets, have not been developed within the Internet - yet.

- **Shift from utilitarian to value-added services:** IT has been both a friend and a foe of private banking services. It has reduced certain core products to utilitarian status such as broking where the execution of trades has been reduced almost to cheque-processing status. The clear divide that is emerging between utilitarian services and value-added services will force providers to review fundamentally what they provide, what they provide in-house and what they charge on the basis of value as perceived by the client. The increasing focus today in the provision of wealth management services is on valuable information, improving proprietary products and performance and on how technology can achieve these end results.

- **Extending the focus to revenue generation:** On the whole, the industry has been slow to embrace the role of technology in supporting revenue generation. The recent focus within the industry has been on cost reduction and cost management in particular, and on automating processes as well as upgrading portfolio management. The role of technology ought to shift firmly to data capture and management in order to assist relationship management and client acquisition. A striking contrast is with the credit card industry that hoards and analyses every scrap of information on its market to understand and to better target its existing and new clients, turning what was previously thought of as 'dumb' data into useable data. Admittedly, there is now growing recognition within the industry that formal client management systems are an essential part of the future. How extensively these systems are adopted and developed will depend on overcoming barriers of a cultural nature and on the individual manager's ability to keep up with and manage the technology. The availability of technology is not an answer, it is the ability to use it effectively that remains key.

- **Strategic role in the re-invention of private banking providers:** Advances in information technology mean that providers have the opportunity to be more radical and innovative in how they grasp the future opportunity. The key is to achieve business focus at a time when providers throughout the industry are extending themselves beyond their natural constituencies. Now more than at any other time, with specialisation in products and processing, providers need to review their area of expertise and evaluate the services and functions best supported from within and what can be bought or sourced from outside. So far, typical areas for out-sourcing are investment research, custody, IT operations and banking back offices. Will more radical areas such as products and fund management be out-sourced more in the future? This ought to be considered because the advances in technology will allow providers to focus on achieving best quality for the client.

Service delivery and business standards

There are some key facts about service in the private banking industry:[4]

- Sixty per cent of costs relate to people.
- Service is considered the number-one recruitment device over the next five years.
- Private bankers spend nearly half of their time with existing clients and a quarter of their time prospecting for new clients.
- Service quality is considered by the industry one of the most pressing issues for today and over the next five years.

Nevertheless, some important issues need to be addressed with regard to service quality and the achievement of business standards.

- **There is a pressing need for a clearer articulation of service:** Some of the providers are so big that it is hard to believe that personal service is always available. Added to this is the diversity of servicing requirements, from very active to passive, the growing use of personal computers and on-line facilities, and a strong client preference for having a number of financial advisers. It puts servicing under the spotlight but even more so the need for a clearly defined, segmented, measurable and monitored range of servicing programmes. These will inevitably include a variety of tools, from formal prospecting, client servicing programmes and disinvestment programmes to independent research on the providers' delivery of service.

- **Growing opportunity to use performance management and remuneration to foster accountability and performance:** Where significant change is required, there is scope to use remuneration and reward structures in more innovative and facilitative ways. Remuneration and reward can be a significant aid to change and drive business forward. The issue within private banking is how to retain high achievers, address the skill shortage already apparent, and the gaps that are opening up in remuneration levels among providers within both international and domestic sectors. Private banking providers will need to explore further the use of performance measurement tools and remuneration even if it is only to keep their staff and ward off predators.
- **Career structures and flattening organisation structures:** Across organisations worldwide, it is a general trend that structures are flattening with the removal of multiple layers. The diminishing hierarchy compounds the already evident problem within private banking concerning career progression, or rather the apparent lack of it. Private banking is not untypical of other lines of business where staff still aspire to the more traditional aspects of career progression such as promotion, status and seniority. Although the overriding service characteristic of private banking is continuity of the private banker, the promise of a job for life is no longer there, and remuneration and motivation for retention have to come in other forms that can address both the organisation's, the individual's and the client's needs.

New competencies and measures of success

The private banking industry has always been valued by clients for safety, security and stability. However, providers increasingly are going to be measured according to a set of new criteria that also include a provider's ability to address and manage change effectively. The core competencies should now focus more tightly on profitability, business activity measures, product quality and risk management. The ability to deliver these will distinguish the winners.

- **Not size but profit and shareholder value:** Importantly, success will be measured not on size alone but also on quality. While size bestows a number of advantages, focus bestows even more, and the market is large enough and discerning enough to accommodate specialisation as well as the universal and large provider. The habitual measurement of funds under management may well be an indicator of market share but it is too one-dimensional and does not reflect the changed dynamics of client retention, revenue enhancement, cost management and shareholder value.
- **A new range of business measures that address both productivity and results:** It will not be sufficient to look at office and team productivity alone. Measurement needs to be extended to fully embrace profitability by client, looking at: cost - income ratios; client satisfaction, using objective tools; how much of a client's overall wealth is under management; client retention; and cross-selling programmes. Furthermore, business growth and specifically the control and influence of the referral channel and referral marketing are increasingly important, given the predicted revenue growth rates and the re-balancing of revenue towards new clients. Prospecting and channel management measures will need to be included too.
- **Not just breadth and depth of product range but performance and quality:** Shifts in attitudes towards product quality are already identifiable in both clients and intermediaries such as trustees. It is in the field of investment management where the issue of performance and quality is complex and topical. Industry views diverge as to whether independent performance measurement will happen and, if it does, whether it is desirable. Undoubtedly, if it happens, it will lead to a more standardised approach to investment management. What is not clear is how much the clients themselves are driving this issue. Certainly the market trend as far as clients are concerned is for more information and transparency as awareness and sophistication levels rise. Whether the desire for information stems from dissatisfaction about performance, and whether the solution resides in composite performance measurement, is another issue. Commitment to such a

programme requires extensive changes and is one for the long term. However, it must make sense at an individual provider level to have quantifiable benchmarks with which to satisfy clients across a range of indicators. If performance against these indicators has been assessed independently, so much the better.

- **Preservation and enhancement of the provider's reputation through effective risk management:** Private banking providers have an expanding risk-management role across financial markets, lending and the regulatory environment. A continuing trend will be the central management of a provider's risk and financial market exposure through focused and dedicated investment strategy teams, which provide the guidelines and parameters for portfolio managers. Generally, the provision of credit will continue to be an important part of the product portfolio although demand for it will vary in strength from market to market. Secured lending will continue to be more typical where clients are seeking to maximise wealth. The regulatory tide is not expected to abate. Risk within certain product categories is becoming more apparent, for example in relation to trusts, particularly where the drawing-up of the original trust might come into question and private bankers find themselves working in a more litigious environment. Furthermore, providers may well start taking stronger positions with regard to higher-risk products particularly when considering what is truly in the client's best interest. Money laundering and due diligence will continue to be a pressing issue and one which will require careful judgement. Regulations and their growing number as well as the lack of regulations in certain jurisdictions will continue to be of central importance in the future.

But perspectives are important too. What was said in 1930 by John Maynard Keynes, is said today, and will be said again tomorrow: 'We are suffering, not from the rheumatics of old age, but from the growing pains of over-rapid changes, from the painfulness of readjustment between one economic period and another. The increase of technical efficiency has been taking place faster than we can deal with the problem of labour absorption.'

Change management will be an integral part of the life of private banking, whereas traditionally the industry has been rewarded for its enduring stability. The challenges for the future are those within the areas of predicted change that a private banking provider will have to face. But then, of course, there is always the unpredictable.

Notes

1 'The evolving global economy, Making sense of the New World Order', edited by Kenichi Ohmae, *Harvard Business Review*, 1995.
2 'Economic globalisation marches on like it or not', *Business Times*, 20 February 1997.
3 'Analysts roundup - analysts question technology spending', *American Banker*, 12 April 1996, p. 14; 'Technology in Finance', Survey, *The Economist*, 26 October 1996; *European Private Banking Survey, 1996/1997*, Price Waterhouse, p. 30.
4 *European Private Banking Survey, 1996/1997*, Price Waterhouse.

Index